Stories Behind the Gospel!

50
Southern Gospel
Favorites

Lindsay Terry

FOREWORD BY GEORGE YOUNCE

Kregel
Publications

Stories Behind 50 Southern Gospel Favorites, Volume 1

© 2002 by Lindsay Terry

Published by Kregel Publications, a division of Kregel, Inc., P.O. Box 2607, Grand Rapids, MI 49501. Kregel Publications provides trusted, biblical publications for Christian growth and service. Your comments and suggestions are valued.

All rights reserved. No part of this book may be reproduced, stored in a retrieval system, or transmitted in any form or by any means—electronic, mechanical, photocopy, recording, or otherwise—without written permission of the publisher, except for brief quotations in printed reviews.

Unless otherwise indicated, Scripture quotations are from the King James version of the Holy Bible.

For more information about Kregel Publications, visit our Web site: www.kregel.com.

Library of Congress Cataloging-in-Publication Data
Stories behind 50 southern gospel favorites, volume 1 / by Lindsay Terry; foreword by George Younce.
   p.   cm.
Includes bibliographical references and index.
   1. Hymns, English—History and criticism. I. Title: Stories behind fifty southern gospel favorites. II. Title.
BV315 .T46   2002   264'.23—dc21
2002011859

ISBN 0-8254-3819-5

Printed in the United States of America

02 03 04 05 06 / 5 4 3 2 1

This book is affectionately dedicated to the memory of Marvin J. Terry Sr. and Myrtle P. Terry, my parents, who are now with the Lord. My dad was especially fond of Southern Gospel Music. As a child, I often heard him singing tunes that were popular during those days, and I was impressed with the quality of his voice. They were wonderful parents, and I am deeply grateful for their love and for all of the opportunities they afforded me.

Contents

Part 2: A Special Section of Classic Hymns and Gospel Songs Often Recorded and Sung by Southern Gospel Groups

Foreword

It's exciting when singers discover a beautiful new song—from either an aspiring songwriter or someone who's written many favorites. It's even more exciting to share these new songs with audiences. To learn how the songs came into being makes the experience complete. You'll be surprised and enlightened, and your heart will be warmed as you read these unusual stories—stories behind the Southern Gospel songs we love.

For the past fifty-four years the Lord has allowed me to spread His Word through song in the form of Southern Gospel Music. As members of the Cathedral Quartet, my associates and I have been voices for channeling the soul-stirring musical messages of these songwriters. I've had the privilege, too, of singing and recording some of the most popular Southern Gospel songs written by many of our most gifted songwriters, most of whom are included in this book. It's been a wonderful musical journey!

So when my friend Lindsay Terry approached me to write the foreword for his book, I was extremely honored. I have enormous respect and admiration for the songwriters whose stories are told in this volume. They have written songs that are not only Southern Gospel "favorites," but what I believe to be "classics." These songs have influenced thousands of lives, and you'll be touched by the stories behind them.

Lindsay has done a masterful job of assembling insightful pictures into the events and human experiences that led to the writing of these Southern Gospel favorites. I know you'll immensely enjoy this book.

—George Younce

Preface

Out of a period of darkness sprang a sunbeam—a song. Most of the Southern Gospel songs that minister to people—and have stood the test of time—were born out of human suffering.

I began interviewing songwriters in 1958, starting with Mosie Lister in Tampa, Florida. Since then I've talked with scores of composers, getting their stories by phone or in person. The stories reveal something of the lives and backgrounds of the writers—who are as different as snowflakes. Almost all of them, however, take little or no credit for what they consider gifts from God. This volume is another in the growing number of books that I've written and continue to write, recording these fascinating stories.

Some of the songs that have become international favorites were written by the singers who helped make them popular. On the other hand, hundreds of meaningful compositions were written by ordinary people, living ordinary lives, but with extraordinary talent for putting onto paper what was in their hearts. Some of the stories are comical, some are sad, some are heartwarming, but all are true—true stories about God's people who are willing to be used of Him to bless the hearts of others.

Acknowledgments

$\mathcal{I}$ thank the talented, dedicated songwriters who so graciously gave me their stories, without which this book would not be possible. It is my goal to show you their "hearts" in this volume.

I appreciate the work of Jim Weaver of Kregel Publications for believing in this project and for presenting it to the people at Kregel. The time we spent discussing the manuscript at my home on Anastasia Island, near St. Augustine, Florida, was greatly helpful and enjoyable. His suggestions were valued. Thanks to Dave Hill, Dennis Hillman, Sarah De Mey, and Janyre Tromp of Kregel Publications for their encouragement and their cheerful attitudes.

My daughter-in-law, Becky Terry, did mountains of work in transcribing the taped interviews. She is a court reporter who is taking time out of her promising career to be a stay-at-home mom to three precious little girls. Thanks, also, to my son, Lance, who, although very busy in his chiropractic clinic, helped out with the children while Becky worked on this project.

My wife, Marilyn, made valuable contributions, proofing and offering wise suggestions, making the stories more readable and interesting.

Thanks to Belinda Flores and Lisa Kerr for work on their computers, which aided in the completion of this book.

My appreciation to Gloria Gaither for allowing me to use information about "The Family of God" from her book, *Fully Alive*, copyright 1984, by Gloria Gaither, published by Gaither Music Company. I received bits of information about "The Old

Rugged Cross" from the Internet and from Alfred B. Smith's book, *Hymn Histories,* copyright 1981, Greenville, South Carolina. Concerning "Blessed Assurance," I received helpful information—which completed other facts obtained from several sources—from *Hymns of Faith,* by Pamela J. Kennedy, copyright 1990, by Ideals Publications, Inc., Nashville, Tennessee. Information concerning Albert Brumley was received from his son and from a newspaper article, "A Hymn Is Born," by Clint Bonner, published in the mid-1900s.

Introduction

A Brief History of Southern Gospel Music

*W*hen we think of Southern Gospel Music, many names immediately come to mind—Mosie Lister, George Younce, Bill and Gloria Gaither, Jake Hess, Naomi Sego Reader, Dottie Rambo, Calvin Wills, and Howard and Vestal Goodman. These are only a few of the many well-known personalities of this genre of Christian music. They, along with hundreds of others, carry on a tradition that had its beginning in the mid-1800s.

During those early years Ephraim Ruebush and Aldine Kieffer were most active in the spread of Southern Gospel Music, as it came to be called. Ruebush and Kieffer were the originators of a scale that allowed for a more complete harmony in the arranging of songs. Until that time many southern songs were sung using a scale of four notes, which came to be known as Sacred Harp. Kieffer and Ruebush used seven shaped notes to denote each pitch on the scale. Students of gospel music were taught in "singing schools" to use that method, and some music is still published today in shaped-note form.

James D. Vaughn was another major player in the development of Southern Gospel Music. Credited with having started the traveling quartet movement, he was also a publisher of song books. Some call Vaughn the "father" of Southern Gospel Music, while others use the term "founder."

During the years that followed Ruebush and Kieffer's development of the shaped-note scale, singing schools became very popular, especially in rural communities. They were often held in churches or other common meeting places, and people who wanted to learn the shaped-note system of singing flocked to those "schools." Albert Brumley taught more than fifty of these singing schools before devoting himself full-time to the writing of songs. His first published song was "I'll Fly Away" in 1931. In the early to mid-1900s, Brumley was the most prolific Southern Gospel songwriter in America. Traveling quartets and radio programs carried his musical messages across our nation, and researchers for the Smithsonian Institute called him "the greatest white gospel songwriter before World War II."

E. M. Bartlett Sr., who died in 1941, was the founder of the Hartford Music Company and the Hartford Musical Institute, which launched the careers of many successful writers and teachers. Bartlett wrote hundreds of songs, including "Victory in Jesus."

It would be remiss not to mention some other pioneers of Southern Gospel Music—V. O. Stamps, Frank Stamps, James Blackwood, Lee Roy Abernathy, G. T. "Dad" Speer, Hovie Lister, J. D. Sumner, and Bob Wills. Others, just as talented and influential, could be added to the list.

Since shortly after the turn of the twentieth century, Southern Gospel Music has seen unusual acceptance and appreciation. But in the past two or three decades the growth and popularity of the songs and the traveling groups who sing them have been phenomenal. From the first traveling quartet, in the mid-1800s— made up of James D. Vaughn and three of his brothers—the number of singing groups in the United States may now number as many as eight thousand. Today, thousands of dedicated young people are enthusiastically involved with Southern Gospel Music, indicating that the tide will continue to swell. Some of these are part-time groups that sing for special occasions and on weekends, while others keep a full schedule all through the year.

The Gaither Homecoming videos and concerts have created

a stir in our nation, causing interest in Southern Gospel Music to skyrocket. The renewed interest has helped many of the older Southern Gospel greats to become even more recognized and popular. Some who had left the "road" have been called back out and are now appearing regularly in concerts. A prime example is James Vaughn Hill, former member of the Stamps Quartet and the Statesmen Quartet, and composer of "What a Day That Will Be." His story, along with those of others, is included in this volume.

Part 1

Stories of Southern Gospel Songs

1

Standing with the Family

The Family of God

1 John 4:7-21

*Beloved, if God so loved us, we ought also to love
one another.*

$\mathcal{G}$od has given only a few people an ability to compose song after song that combines beautiful lyrics and infectious, singable melodies. Such are the Gaithers. For nearly forty years, Bill and Gloria Gaither have influenced the singing of Christians around the world. Major tools for doing so have been their recording of dozens of albums, CDs, and videos. An indication of their influence and acceptance is their numerous Dove and Grammy Awards. The Gospel Music Association named them Songwriter of the Year nine times. Gloria has written numerous books, and Bill and Gloria have cowritten at least ten major musicals. Their music publishing companies have for many years circulated their music and books around the world.

If you haven't seen one of the Gaither Homecoming concerts on television, or viewed a Homecoming video—the sales of which number into the millions—then you are likely out of touch with the Christian music world. Thousands flock to their live concerts, which are videotaped in scores of cities across America. Their music is bringing another generation of music fans into the Southern Gospel Music fold.

They seem always open to the leading of the Holy Spirit in the writing of a song. One of the Gaithers' most meaningful and widely used songs, written in 1970, was born out of hardship and trial, as are many of the most beloved hymns and gospel songs.

The Gaithers are members of a local church in Alexandria, Indiana, and the church body is very dear to them. A young family in their congregation, Ron and Darlene Garner and their three children, inspired the writing of the Gaithers' song "The Family of God," according to Gloria Gaither in her book *Because He Lives* ([Old Tappan, N.J.: Revell, 1988], 123–29).

"The Saturday after Good Friday Ron went to the garage where he worked as a mechanic. He was working alone that day because he was making up time that he had taken off the previous Thursday. He'd taken his little daughter for some tests prior to some anticipated heart surgery. With the operation coming up, he knew they'd need the money for hospital and doctor bills. While Ron was working with combustible material, there was an explosion. He managed to crash his way through the large double doors before the building blew apart and went up in flames, but he was severely burned over most of his body.

"The news from the emergency ward in Muncie was pessimistic: Ron was alive but was not expected to make it through the night. It was only minutes before a chain of telephone calls alerted the family of God, and the whole church began to pray for Ron. All day long they prayed. Little groups, bigger groups, in homes, at the church, over the phone—all over town the people who were related to Ron and Darlene because of Jesus prayed. By evening the word came—the doctors gave no hope, but Ron was still alive. They couldn't understand how he was holding on, but now that he had lived eight hours, possibly, if he could make it until morning, there was a chance—just a chance.

"The Family kept on praying. Old folks prayed alone in their rooms. Children prayed in simple faith. Women prayed as they went about the tasks of caring for their families. Men prayed together in basements and over store counters and in automobiles. The church building was kept open, and lights burned all through the night as a steady stream of folks who cared and loved came to talk to Jesus about this young father who was 'bone of their bone and flesh of their flesh.'

"The sun streamed in the windows that Easter morning on a sanctuary filled with the most weary, bleary-eyed congregation you've ever seen. There were very few Easter bonnets or bright new outfits. We were just there, drawn together closer than we'd ever been before by the reality we shared—that when one part of the body suffers, we all suffer.

"Nobody felt like celebrating. There was hurt and there was pain in the body, and that pain had drawn the attention of every other member.

"About twenty minutes into the service, the pastor came in with a report from the hospital. Although he had gone without sleep to be with the Garner family through the long hours, there was sunshine in his eyes. 'Ron has outlived the deadline. The doctors say he has a chance. They're going to begin treatment.'

"For the body of Christ, that news was better than eight hours of sleep and a good breakfast. New life was infused into us all. Tears of praise and joy began to flow, and our hope and gratitude poured itself into the glorious songs of Easter. 'Jesus lives, and because He lives, we too shall live!'

"Those songs that day were for us songs of commitment, too. We knew that the long, hard days for Ron and Darlene and the children had only just begun. With the words of victory we pledged ourselves to what would lie ahead: help with the children, many long trips to the hospital, pints of blood for transfusions, money for the astronomic hospital bills, meals to be taken to the family who would be too tired to cook, long months of support while the slow skin grafting and healing process went on. We knew what it would mean, and in our celebration we pledged ourselves to whatever it would take to make that injured part of the body whole and well again.

"On our way home from church that morning we [Bill and I] were so full of the beauty of it all that we could hardly speak. Finally, we said to each other what we had come to realize through all this: 'They'd do that for us, too!' It was almost too grand to realize, but it was true! We aren't very model church members. The function we fill in the body of Christ takes us away from a lot of the activities of our congregation. We're never available on Fridays and Saturdays. We get in early on Sunday mornings in time to get our children ready and to their Sunday school and church, but we can't be counted on to teach a class with a schedule like that.

"We always miss the fish fries, and I'm never there to make cakes and pies for the bake sales. But they'd do the same thing for us if we were the part of the body that was suffering! Not because we were worthy or had earned special treatment or were indispensable—but just because we were a part of the family of God!

"As I started dinner, Bill sat down at the piano. (The children were quiet, knowing that a song was about to be born.) It wasn't long before the magnetism of the chorus Bill was singing drew me from the kitchen to the piano, and we finished the song that was to feed us better than any other food could have fed us."

In the lyrics, the Gaithers express their joy at being part of the "family of God." They cleverly included in the text the message of salvation through the blood of Christ, as well as a description of our relation to Christ as "joint heirs." They make it sound wonderful—and it is—to be part of the "family of God."

Gloria continues, "Since that Easter Sunday there have been heartaches and victories in our own lives that have been shared by the family of God. It's been wonderful. Ron is a very healthy, robust basketball coach these days. His life is a strong witness in our community to the power and love of Christ."

21

Reflection

Apart from our salvation, the most wonderful gifts from God are Christian brothers and sisters who love us and who are loved by us in full measure as part of His family.

2

A Moment of Truth

Greater Is He That Is in Me

1 John 4:1-6

Ye are of God, little children, and have overcome them: because greater is he that is in you, than he that is in the world.

$\mathscr{L}$anny Wolfe, born on February 2, 1942, is one of the most educated songwriters of our day. He holds four degrees, two bachelor's degrees and two master's degrees, from such schools as Ohio State University, San Jose State University, and Southern Illinois University. He has written approximately three hundred songs, most of them published.

He confesses that although his first two degrees were in another direction—a bachelor of science degree in business education and a master's degree in business administration—he still had music in his "gut." He wanted to be involved with music, but had no background. That lack led him to the Western Apostolic Bible College in California for one year before entering San Jose State.

Lanny says that one of his most famous songs, "Greater Is He That Is in Me," came in response to a moment of truth. He says, "I had read that Scripture [1 John 4:4] many times, but it wasn't special until a certain time when I was riding in a car, traveling through Nevada, while going up to Montana. It was a moment when that Scripture, as I thought of it, became so real—the amazing fact that Christ lives within us and that He is so much more powerful and greater than the one who rules the affairs of the unsaved people of this world. Imagine—He lives within us and he is omnipotent!

"During those times I never wrote out songs. I just kept them in my head. Our singing group would learn a song by having me sing it to them in a studio situation. It would then be written down so that it might be published. During those studio sessions, we were able to hone it and make what corrections seemed necessary. That procedure happened with 'Greater Is He That Is in Me,' and that's how the song came into being."

Repeating twice the first line of the chorus, "Greater Is He That Is in Me," seals the message into our hearts and minds.

In the first verse, Lanny warns of Satan's attempts to conquer Christians in their weakest hours. But, he adds, we can be victorious through the power of God's Word.

In the second verse, Lanny reminds us of the coming of the Holy Spirit on the Day of Pentecost and that He abides in us today, causing us to be victorious in Christ.

Reflection

What a marvelous existence we enjoy as children of God. Our Lord, with all of His omnipotence and His glory, actually dwells within our hearts. What protection, what security, and what joy!

3

A Musical Good-bye

If We Never Meet Again

John 14:1–6

*And if I go and prepare a place for you, I will come
again, and receive you unto myself; that where I
am, there ye may be also.*

$\mathcal{A}$lbert Brumley was one of the great Southern Gospel
songwriters of all time. His songs reverberated across America
in the early 1930s, encouraging millions of people who endured
extremely difficult times during the Great Depression. For
Southern Gospel Music lovers, Brumley was the "Mosie Lister"
of the thirties and forties.

Born to William and Sarah Brumley near Spiro, Oklahoma,
on October 29, 1905, young Albert began his study of music as
a lad of seventeen, attending singing schools and music normal
schools. He attended the Hartford Music Institute, Hartford,
Arkansas, from 1926 to 1931, and also studied under such music greats as Homer Rodeheaver, E. M. Bartlett, Virgil O. Stamps,
and Dr. J. B. Herbert.

Many of the themes of Brumley's songs came out of his days
growing up on a cotton farm, and his early efforts at songwriting
were mostly for his own pleasure. It was not until he met and
married Goldie Schell that he began to have his music published—a direct result of her encouragement. His first published

song was "I'll Fly Away," and from that point on he devoted more time to songwriting.

He sang with the Hartford Quartet for a time, but in those days it was hard for a full-time traveling quartet to make a living. So he soon left that employment to teach music and to tune pianos. Plus, he also taught at a total of fifty-one singing schools and music normal schools in Arkansas, Oklahoma, and Missouri.

During his more than twenty years of appearing at song gatherings and all-day singings, he found it increasingly difficult to say good-bye to the crowds who had gathered and sang his songs for hours. Clint Bonner, syndicated newspaper columnist during the mid-1900s, quoted Brumley in his article "A Hymn Is Born": "It does something to you when people sing your songs for two hours and then hundreds of them come down front to shake your hand. There are dear old souls with tears in their eyes who tell you how they love to sing 'I Dreamed I Met Mother and Daddy.' There are those who have lost loved ones, and they want to talk about 'I'll Meet You in the Morning.'"

Bonner explains that Brumley devised a unique way to tell audiences "Good-bye." He wrote a song to sing with the people at the close of concerts and all-day singings. The song not only closed the gatherings, but it became so popular that it sold in sheet music form and was also translated into several other languages.

The song—"If We Never Meet Again."

In the lyrics, Brumley comforts Christians who find it necessary to part from loved ones and friends, perhaps never again to meet on this earth. He explains that the sorrow and pain felt here on earth will be non-existent in heaven.

His own good-byes to those who had participated in the "singings" were expressed in the closing line of his song.

Reflection

The promise of a "better place" after our lives on this earth are ended explains the popularity of hundreds of songs about heaven. The prospect of living in the presence of Christ, as we gather around His throne with the loved ones and friends we've known down here, makes saying good-bye a little easier.

4

A Pioneer Leaves a Song

The Eastern Gate

Psalm 30

*For his anger endureth but a moment; in his
favour is life: weeping may endure for a night, but
joy cometh in the morning.*

The small town of Kirksville, Missouri, was the birthplace of
one of the great songwriters of years gone by. The Reverend
I. G. Martin was born on April 18, 1862, and became a Christian at a very early age. Sometime after his conversion, however, he drifted away from his commitment to the Lord.

After receiving his college training, Martin became a teacher,
but this vocation was short-lived. Young Martin then turned his
attention to the stage, where he performed as an actor and
singer, a profession that led him further away from his commitment to Christ.

Years later, he one day found himself in a revival service in
Milwaukee, Wisconsin. The services were led by a Methodist
evangelist named Tillotsen, and P. P. Bilhorn was the singer
and song leader. After hearing the preaching and singing of
those revivalists, Martin rededicated his life to Christ and determined to serve the Lord again. He later entered the ministry as an evangelistic singer.

Martin soon began to preach as well as to sing. His travels

carried him to many places in our nation where he spoke and sang in churches and camp meetings. During these years of ministry, he began writing songs—songs that seemed to flow eloquently from his soul.

In the early years of the Church of the Nazarene, Martin was appointed by Dr. Bresee as superintendent of the eastern district, which consisted of the territory east of the Rocky Mountains. For six years Martin served the First Nazarene Church in Chicago and later moved to Malden, Massachusetts.

Martin lived for nearly a century, passing away in August 1967. Haldor Lillenas, who knew Martin for a portion of the more than fifty years that he preached the gospel, said, "He was indeed one of the staunch pioneers of our church. He lived long and well, loved his Lord fervently, served his church faithfully, and was a devoted husband and father."

Millions of Christians are glad that before he departed this life, I. G. Martin wrote a beautiful song about heaven. And so, happily, we sing "The Eastern Gate."

> I will meet you in the morning,
> Just inside the Eastern Gate,
> Then, be ready faithful pilgrim,
> Lest for you it be too late.
>
> Chorus:
> I will meet you, I will meet you,
> Just inside the Eastern Gate over there.
> I will meet you, I will meet you,
> I will meet you in the morning over there.
>
> O the joys of that glad meeting,
> With the saints who for us wait,
> What a blessed happy meeting,
> Just inside the Eastern Gate.

In recent years this song has experienced a revival in popularity, and it has become a favorite of thousands of Christians.

Reflection

When our loved ones are taken into the arms of God, joy and peace unspeakable should flood our very souls as we anticipate the reunion in heaven.

5

A Rare Sunday at Home

Canaanland Is Just in Sight

Joshua 1:1–9

*Be strong and of a good courage; be not afraid,
neither be thou dismayed: for the LORD thy God is
with thee whithersoever thou goest.*

A trivia question: He traveled for twenty-one years with an outstanding singing group based in North Carolina. During that time the group recorded fourteen albums and CDs. He wrote all of the songs on all of their recordings, which totaled 140 compositions. At least one of his songs has been sung by the Mormon Tabernacle Choir, and one of his songs was named Song of the Year. Who is he? If your answer is Jeff Gibson, then you're correct!

Jeffrey Gibson's story is inspirational, but the story behind his most famous song is provocative. Jeff was born to J. T. and Ernestine "Pauli" Gibson in Rocky Mount, North Carolina, in 1955. He says, "I began to have a real interest in church music at the age of nine, singing and playing the piano. I was still very young when the pianist at our church, the Church of God in Enfield, North Carolina, moved away and I was asked to accompany the choir.

"I was only ten years old when I turned my heart over to Christ. The pastor of the small church, with about fifty to sixty people present, leaned over to me and said, 'The Lord is really going to do something with you now.' At that young age I thought, 'Well, OK!' I never understood why God chose to use me, and I still don't, but I am grateful.

"When I was in my early teens our youth group became weary of the old hymns we used in the church, so I began to write songs for them. I would also write for small groups in our church. That's how my songwriting began.

"During high school I learned to play guitar, drums, trumpet, saxophone, and clarinet. By the time I got out of high school I was granted a music scholarship to Atlantic Christian College in Wilson, North Carolina. During my college years I increased in my ability to play several instruments to the point that I was able to teach others to play them. My goal was to teach music when I graduated from college, but the Lord had other plans for me.

"After receiving my degree, instead of teaching school I joined a Southern Gospel quartet called Heaven Bound and sang baritone in the group for twenty-one years. I had the privilege of writing all of the songs that we recorded in those years—fourteen albums and CDs with ten songs on each of them.

"On a particular Sunday in 1983, Heaven Bound had a Sunday off, which was very rare, so we attended our home church. As I sat in Pastor Jim Forehand's Sunday school class that morning, I heard him teach about the children of Israel and their journey through the wilderness. As he told of their hardships and the encouragement of Moses, the thought occurred to me, *Moses must have urged them many times to just hang on because Canaanland is just in sight.* This sparked an idea for a song and so I began to write. In only a few minutes I had completed the song, right there in the class. The pastor later said, 'I saw that you were distracted, but I knew you were writing a song.'

"I was so excited about it, I sang it quietly to my wife, Bern, as we walked down the hallway from the Sunday school classroom to the church auditorium for the morning service. When I reached the auditorium I quickly went over to Ken Eubanks, the pianist for Heaven Bound, and said, 'Ken, the Lord has just given me a song. I really believe He is going to use it.' And so I sang it to him, 'There will be no sorrow, there in that tomorrow. . . .'

"Later that afternoon, back on the bus with Heaven Bound going to another concert, Ken said, 'Jeff sing me that song again that the Lord gave you this morning.' Well, I sang it for all of the guys and we learned it that very afternoon. I said, 'This will be a great song for the Cathedrals or the Kingsmen,' but the guys said, 'No, no, that's our song!' We recorded it a few weeks later.

"The other groups picked it up from our recording and began to use it. At my last count 632 groups and soloists had recorded it. I finally said, 'I can't keep up with this.' And so I quit counting, therefore, I don't know how many people have recorded it.

"I've gotten letters and testimonials from numbers of people that have been blessed by the song, but one letter that is so meaningful to me came from Africa. A missionary there was about to preach his first sermon in Africa. He and his wife were so afraid and nervous. He quickly prayed, 'God give me something in my heart to make me feel at home. Please make my wife and me to be at ease.' Presently an African choir began to sing 'Canaanland Is Just in Sight.' The missionary said, 'Immediately the Lord gave us peace.'

"An elderly gentleman walked up to me once and said, 'I just appreciate so much the song 'Canaanland Is Just in Sight,' and I want to give you something. He extended his opened hand and I saw fourteen cents, 'This isn't much' he said, 'but it's all that I have and I want to give you this to thank you for the song.' I was hesitant to take it, but I didn't want to offend him. That kind and heartwarming expression of gratitude for my song meant more to me than anybody will ever know."

Those occasions, Jeff proclaims, mean more to him than all of the awards.

Jeff Gibson has had more than 250 of his songs published or recorded. He said of his songwriting, "Like any other writer, I have a drawer full of songs that nobody has ever heard, so I don't know just how many songs I've actually written."

"Canaanland" has not only been sung to millions of people by traveling groups, but has also been published in song books and choral collections, causing it to be a blessing to many more thousands of people.

Jeff left the Heaven Bound quartet to devote more time to writing songs, and at the time of this writing, Jeff Gibson is a music teacher for a middle school in Kinston, North Carolina. In the year 1999 he was Teacher of the Year for his school and went on to win that honor countywide and then statewide. Jeff has limited involvement, however, in the music in his local church.

Reflection

We learn a tremendous spiritual lesson from "Canaanland." We live by faith and we just keep moving forward for the Lord. With His help and grace we can keep putting one foot in front of the other until victory comes, or until we rest in Him, *"looking unto Jesus the author and finisher of our faith"* (Heb. 12:2).

6

A Record, Not Yet Broken

Rise Again

Matthew 28:1–10

*He is not here: for he is risen, as he said. Come, see
the place where the Lord lay. And go quickly, and
tell his disciples that he is risen from the dead.*

$\mathcal{D}$allas Holm declares that in his fantasy life he would be a
frontiersman. His passion for the outdoors—hunting, fishing,
and camping—leads him to jest that maybe he was born a few
hundred years too late. This ministry-minded songwriter and
performer was born in 1948 to Howard and Viola Holm, in
St. Paul, Minnesota. He has influenced the Christian music world
with his songs, becoming the first contemporary artist to win
Dove Awards for Song of the Year, Songwriter of the Year, and
Male Vocalist of the Year. One of his songs, "Rise Again," has set
"chart records" that have not been surpassed for more than a
quarter century and counting. More about that song later.

Although Dallas was raised by Christian parents, by age sixteen he was playing in rock bands for dances and parties that
they could never approve of. So on Sunday evening, October
17, 1965, Pastor Dick Dresselhaus of the Summit Avenue Assembly of God in St. Paul talked to young Dallas about his life.
Holm knew that he needed to be changed, and when confronted
with the claims of the Bible he made the decision to trust Jesus

Christ as his personal Savior. Dallas said, "When I became a Christian, along with the commitment of my life to the Lord was a commitment of my music—I would only write for Him."

He said, "My interest as a young Christian was in contemporary music. I felt that there must be some way to use drums and electric guitars to serve the Lord. At that time the term 'Contemporary Christian Music' had not even been invented, but I remember going to jails, rest homes, street corners, and small conservative churches in the St. Paul area to present the 'praise' music of our small band. On more than one occasion our engagements were cut short in churches by the pastors who would graciously explain why we couldn't or shouldn't do that kind of music in church. I grew up in an area populated with many conservative Scandinavians, Norwegians, and Swedes, and it was unheard of to use drums and electric guitars in their churches."

In 1970, David Wilkerson, made famous by his book, *The Cross and the Switchblade*, asked Dallas to join him in his youth crusade ministry as soloist and song leader. By 1976 they had formed a band called Dallas Holm and Praise as part of the Wilkerson team.

Dallas wrote "Rise Again" in 1976, just after deciding to form the band for the David Wilkerson crusades.

"After we had decided to form the band, I realized that I would need to write some new material. I knew that the music should be different from the things I was used to writing. We would also need arrangements with three-part vocals. So I got out my pen and paper and thought, *I need to get busy and write some songs.* I often had a disciplined approach to songwriting and have written some of my better songs in that frame of mind. But this particular day I couldn't come up with a single idea. I drew an absolute zero.

"I began to pray, which I should have done in the first place, and in the course of my praying I remember saying, 'Lord, if You were singing, what would You sing?' That thought really stuck in my mind. I didn't know if I had ever heard a song from a first-person point of view. As hokey as it may sound, I had this mental image of the Lord, dressed as we often picture Him in our minds, standing on a street corner with a guitar, singing. It was as if you could translate Jesus into modern times, with singing as His form of communication. What would He sing?

"As soon as I focused in on that approach to my task, I began to write as if I were taking dictation. I wrote the music and the words in about ten minutes—no changes. I titled it 'Rise Again.'

"When it was finished I looked at it and realized that this didn't just come out of my head. I have often said that God wrote the song, and I just delivered the message. That describes the way I feel about that experience.

"Dallas Holm and Praise had only been together six weeks when we recorded a 'live' album in the Lindell High School auditorium in Lindell, Texas. It seated about 350 people. We had a mobile unit to come in from Nashville to do the recording, and we spent a whopping $5,000.

"'Rise Again' ended up as 'cut four' on 'side two,' the worst place, and generally referred to as the graveyard of songs. We basically did everything wrong: (1) live albums were not selling; (2) we put the song in the wrong place; and (3) we rushed into the project. We had only been together for a few short weeks. Nevertheless, somewhere, somebody on radio played 'Rise Again,' and word spread. 'Dallas Holm and Praise . . . Live!' went on to be one of the first three albums to receive a Recording Industry Association of America gold-certified record.

"To me it was a great lesson. If God puts His finger on something, and if He anoints it, it doesn't make any difference if all of the right marketing plans and promotional schemes are used. We didn't know anything about that stuff. I think the 'first person' point of view played a great role in the success. Having Christ say, 'Go ahead drive the nails in My hands . . .' impacted the listener.

"*Contemporary Christian Music Magazine* used to have three charts that were categorized as 'Contemporary,' 'Inspirational,' and 'Southern Gospel.' 'Rise Again' was number one on all three of those charts at the same time. As far as we know that has never happened before or since.

"We received a plaque from *Singing News Magazine* for an unprecedented forty-eight months of having 'Rise Again' on their charts. At first I thought they meant weeks, but they said, 'No, it was on the charts for forty-eight months.' Many Southern Gospel quartets recorded and used the song in their concerts."

Dallas is without doubt a gifted songwriter, having written approximately 300 songs, of which more than 250 have been recorded or published. And he has recorded 33 albums and CDs. But his love for motorcycles led him into a wonderful ministry experience. He, along with other members of a Christian motorcycle club take their bikes into prisons, talking with the inmates about them. It allows a tremendous opportunity to witness for Christ.

Blessings on Dallas and his family—Linda and their children, Jennifer and Jeffrey—who are very supportive. Dallas summarizes his goal in life thus: "When I stand before the Lord, it won't be how many records I've sold, or how many people saw me in concert. What we do for Him is never as important as who we are in Him. That's all He's measuring."

Reflection

One compelling event in the earthly life of our Lord makes Him higher and mightier than all others whom some have worshiped. It is His triumph over the tomb. He kept His divine Word to those around Him when He declared, "I will rise again!"

7

A Response to a Television Ad

Champion of Love

Ephesians 2:1–10

*But God, who is rich in mercy, for his great love
wherewith he loved us, even when we were dead in
sins, hath quickened us together with Christ.*

"As soon as I learned to speak I was singing. The earliest memories I have are involved with gospel music," said Phil Cross. Cross is founder and president of Poet Voices, a well-known Southern Gospel quartet, who for the past decade have ministered in churches and concert halls. Cross is a singer-songwriter and excels at both.

He was born to Lawrence and Myrt Cross in Ringgold, Georgia, December 16, 1957. Some of his earliest recollections are singing with his family, the Gospel Sounds. As he grew older his musical experiences included playing drums and studying the guitar. He also took voice lessons at Tennessee Temple University in Chattanooga, Tennessee, not as a full-time student, but in private sessions with Sieglinde Cierpke Brown, an outstanding teacher in the music department.

When Phil was eleven years old, he went to his grandmother's house to spend the night. While there, he came face to face with the fact that he was not a Christian—that he was lost. He told his grandmother that he needed to be saved, and she immediately phoned the preacher. Phil said, "While she was in the other room, making contact with the preacher, I was making contact with God." He came to know Christ personally that night and soon after became a member of the High Point Baptist Church in Apison, Tennessee, near Chattanooga.

Phil began his songwriting ventures at age twenty-three, and to this date has written between 350 and 400 songs, most of which have been recorded or published. His most famous song, "Champion of Love," came to be written in a most imaginative way.

"In the mid-1980s," said Phil, "there was a boxing match being publicized and promoted on television between two champion middle-weight boxers, Sugar Ray Leonard and Marvelous Marvin Hagler. Both fighters were advertised as having never been defeated. The message of the TV ads was that the world must know who is the undisputed, undefeated, middle-weight champion of the world. Those ads went on for weeks. We kept hearing the phrase over and over again—'undisputed, undefeated champion.' It seemed that in almost every other commercial they were saying something about the undisputed, undefeated champions.

"As I listened to the commercials, it occurred to me that one day the world will become aware of whom the all-time, undisputed, undefeated Champion of Love really is. Was His championship temporary, or was it eternal? Was He champion of the world or Champion of heaven? I then asked myself the question, 'If I could introduce Christ as He was, as He is, and as He will always be—the all-time, undisputed, undefeated Champion of Love—how would I do it?'

"I thought, *If I could stand on the highest mountain on earth and could get the attention of the whole world, I would begin the introduction with* . . . 'Ladies and gentlemen, may I have your attention? In this corner of the good and the right stands the Champion, robed in white. . . .'"

Phil thinks he was probably at home when he started the

lyrics, but he's not quite sure. But he's certain that he didn't write it in one sitting.

"It took six months," he said. "I was getting the melody at the same time I was getting the lyrics. That's the way I've always written; they both come at the same time."

After he finished the song, assisted by Carolyn Cross English, he taught it to the Poet Voices, who recorded a demo tape. The tape was sent to Lari Goss, a near-genius of music writing, who wrote "Cornerstone," and who has orchestrated for and directed more recording sessions than any other person in Christian music to date. "Lari took it from there," said Phil.

The song was made popular by the Cathedral Quartet and went on to win a Dove Award as Song of the Year in 1987.

Of all the occasions upon which the song was performed, one of the most notable was Atlanta, Georgia, at the victory celebration when Evander Holyfield retained his heavyweight boxing title. It was reportedly sung by Alvin Slaughter.

The opening phrase "Ladies and gentlemen! May I have your attention?" really gets your attention as the song begins, no matter who sings it. And the unique description of Christ as it unfolds in the verses is outstanding indeed. The song is written so that the chorus rises with layer upon layer of wonderful adulation and praise, finally pronouncing Him "the Champion of Love."

For the past two decades Phil Cross has been recognized as one of this generation's most prolific composers of Southern Gospel Music. He has received numerous awards in recognition of his contributions as a songwriter.

Also known as a master communicator, Phil's insights and humorous stories effectively and dramatically relate the good news of the gospel to his audiences. With a reputation of integrity and dedication to the ministry in which he and Poet Voices are involved, he leads every musical performance, encouraging the saints, and helping point the lost to Christ.

Reflection

Everyone loves a true champion, and it is thrilling to witness the recognition, even in boxing terms, of the omniscience, the omnipotence, and the omnipresence of Jesus Christ. His love was manifested to you and me in a manner that is beyond our finite understanding—His willingness to be crucified to pay our sin debt.

8

A Soon Forgotten Prophecy

Midnight Cry

Matthew 25:1–13

And at midnight there was a cry made, Behold, the
bridegroom cometh; go ye out to meet him. . . .
Watch therefore, for ye know neither the day nor the
hour wherein the Son of man cometh.

"God will give you songs that will change lives." That's what a visiting preacher told seven-year-old Greg Day.

"Just before the benediction," said Greg, "he called me out of the audience and down to the front. I was timid and hesitated, but my mother encouraged me, so I obeyed the preacher. He said to me, 'Son, this may not mean anything to you now, but one day when you are older, God told me to tell you that you will write songs.' I took that as a seven-year-old would. I forgot it."

Greg was born in 1962, to Bob and Grace Day, who taught Greg and his brother Chuck, who was five years older, to play musical instruments. Greg learned piano and Chuck guitar. Greg also played drums, and both became accomplished musicians.

By age twenty-three Greg was an alcoholic. But God began to deal with his heart, and one night in Columbus, Georgia, at 1:30 A.M., after hours of drinking, Greg finally gave in to the conviction of the Holy Spirit and went with Chuck to see the preacher who lived down the road. Chuck had been saved from a life of alcoholism and dope just one month earlier.

"We woke up the preacher," said Greg, "and he led me in a simple sinner's prayer. Jesus delivered me at that moment—instantly." God saved him and immediately freed him from his alcohol addiction, just as He had delivered Chuck a month earlier. Both—delivered instantly!

Some time later, Greg and Chuck paid a visit to their parents in Adel, Georgia. "Their church was beginning a revival on Sunday morning," said Greg, "with a visiting evangelist, Billy Swain, as the preacher for the series of meetings. He had fasted for forty days, preparing himself for the revival. During the fast he had asked God to give him a series of messages on the second coming of Christ. On that first Sunday morning of the campaign he preached the first of his series of sermons called, 'The Midnight Cry.' His text was taken from Matthew, chapter 25.

"Chuck took a business card from his wallet and wrote on it, 'Midnight Cry.' He said to me, 'There's something there.' We continued to listen with interest to the preacher's sermon.

"That afternoon, after lunch with our parents, Chuck and I walked into the living room, and I sat down at the piano. Chuck said, 'You know, we could probably write a song about that sermon—about the midnight cry.' I began to play a few chords on the keyboard. All of a sudden I said, 'I hear the sound of a mighty rushing wind,' and Chuck answered, 'And it's closer now than it's ever been.' Then immediately I came out with, 'I can almost hear the trumpet as Gabriel sounds the call.' Chuck came right back with, 'At the midnight cry we'll be going home.' It was line upon line. I would write a line and he would write a line. That's exactly how 'Midnight Cry' was written—in about thirty minutes total.

"That night at the church Chuck and I sang the song for the first time. We hadn't been singing together so it was a little rough, but the crowd seemed to be very moved.

"My brother and I joined a group called the Accords. I sang with them and he played guitar. After about six months with the Accords, the group had saved enough money from engagements to go to Nashville and record an album. All of the songs had been chosen for the recording sessions—except one. Someone said, 'Let's just do "Midnight Cry," we need another song anyway.' It was almost an afterthought, but it was put into the project.

"Stan Shoeman, who sang in the group, had some experience with 'pitching' songs, so he sent a copy of our album to Gold City in Alabama. It had three or four of his songs on it, plus, of course, 'Midnight Cry.'

"After listening to the tape, Gold City called us and said, 'We like "Midnight Cry" and would like to record it.' We felt badly that they didn't pick any of Stan's songs, but Chuck and I were grateful that he'd done us the favor of including our song on the tape.

"Gold City recorded our song in 1987, with Ivan Parker singing the lead, and sent it out as a 'single.' It hit the charts with such force that it quickly went to number one and stayed in that position on the Singing News charts for a solid six months. 'Midnight Cry' was honored as Song of the Year by Singing News in 1988.

"Billy Swain had asked God to give him a message that would go around the world and tell people of Christ's return. God has done that through 'Midnight Cry.' It's been used or recorded thousands of times and is probably sung every day of the week somewhere in the world. It was even used in the 'Left Behind' movie and video."

After the success of "Midnight Cry," the Spirit reminded Greg of the prophecy the preacher made over him as a lad of seven. Our thanks to Greg Day and Chuck Day who gave to the world such a moving, powerful song. May it be used of the Lord for many years to come.

Today, Greg and his wife, Heather—a singer with the Ruppes—

have a young son, Zachary, who has already sung on a CD with his famous parents. Chuck is a preacher of the gospel, who also has a music ministry and a state-of-the-art recording studio.

Reflection

We often hear of the second coming of Christ. May the truth of His "coming in the clouds" never become commonplace to us. It could happen any day—at morning, noon, or at midnight. And it *will* happen at midnight—somewhere in the world.

9

A Symbol of Christian Liberty

Statue of Liberty

Colossians 1:19–27

. . . having made peace through the blood of his cross,
by him to reconcile all things unto himself . . .

The coveted Dove Award was won in 1974 by a very moving,
thought-provoking song written by Neil Enloe. Then thirty-six,
this singer-songwriter from Wood River, Illinois, had been raised
in a Christian home and started his music-writing career at age
eighteen, about the time he entered Central Bible College. Enloe
had become a Christian just four years earlier.

The song was born out of a sense of allegiance to his Lord
and to his country.

"I was a member of a singing group called the Couriers,
based in Harrisburg, Pennsylvania," said Enloe. "It was in the
early 1970s, and we were scheduled to sing for a boat ride sponsored by a large group of Christian young people from New
York and New Jersey. They had rented a cruise boat for an
evening, and we were to be the musical guests.

"There were twenty-four hundred people on the boat, with
an auditorium that seated only four hundred. We had to sing
six concerts in order for them all to attend during the evening,
and we had only a five-minute break between the concerts.

"During one of the breaks, a member of the group and I

went out on deck and looked at the sights along the shore. By this time it was dark. As I leaned on the ship's rail with my back to the shore, the kids looked excitedly at something and at the same time they oohed and ahhhed. I turned and saw the Statue of Liberty in all her glory, ablaze with lights.

"Because I was raised in the Midwest, everything patriotic in me suddenly rose to the surface. I had never seen it so closely before. It was so very, very close. In my own mind and heart, I realized, anew and afresh, the liberty I have as an American citizen.

"I turned to the fellow with me and said, 'There must be a counterpart to my American freedom—liberty in Christ. There is surely a monument to this liberty!' I thought, *There is no greater symbol to Christian liberty than the cross!*

"I turned to my friend and said, 'There should be a song somewhere in this.'"

After three months of writing and rewriting, Neil Enloe gave to the world his award-winning song, "Statue of Liberty."

In his song he recognizes the "lady" standing in New York harbor, with her torch raised high, as a symbol of the liberty that Americans enjoy. As the lyrics continue he expresses his appreciation for his country.

In the next verse he reminds us that Christ was once lifted high on a cross, and all who look to Him can have liberty that only God can provide. Truly Christ is our liberty and our assurance, and every Christian can claim the cross of Christ as his or her statue of liberty.

Reflection

Christ, and He alone, is our Rescuer. He left His majestic position and condescended through the power of God's love to provide freedom and salvation for lowly human beings. He is to enjoy a place of exaltation in our hearts, for He is King of Kings and Lord of Lords.

10

A Whuppin' for Going to the Other Church

We've Come This Far by Faith

1 Peter 1:6–9

That the trial of your faith, being much more precious than of gold that perisheth, though it be tried with fire, might be found unto praise and honour and glory at the appearing of Jesus Christ.

$\mathcal{A}$s a songwriter Albert Goodson penned only sixteen songs, and only one of those became famous. But as a pianist he has few equals. Goodson, an African-American, is one of twin boys born to Arthur and Clara Goodson in 1933, in Los Angeles, California.

He stated, "I started my interest in music as a child. My parents were too poor to buy a piano, and although my real aspiration was to be a dancer, I would take a wooden board and pretend to play on it as if it were a keyboard. I wanted my brother, Alfred, and me to become a dance team—twin tap dancers. Alfred had no interest in that, but became a jazz musician, mastering the saxophone, while I went toward church music.

"They didn't have a very good choir at the church where my mother insisted that I go, so I would slip away and go to St. Paul Baptist Church, where they had a marvelous pianist, Gwendolyn Cooper, and a two-hundred-voice choir. I had never heard a choir sing like that before. My mother had a cousin who attended the Baptist church and she would say, 'Oh, I saw the twins this morning.' My mother knew she had sent us to the church where she was a member, so I would be punished for sneaking off to the Baptist church, but I would do it about twice a month. When I was much smaller, at times I could lay in my bed in the early evenings and hear the singing of the church choir just down the street. I would crawl out of the window and go closer so that I could hear them better. I would then sneak back in through the window. Mother would sometimes find out about it and give me a whipping.

"I enjoyed listening to the singers at the Baptist church so much they asked me if I wanted to join the choir. I said, 'Yes.' They then asked if I wanted to get baptized. I said, 'Whatever it takes.' And so I got baptized again. I learned everything the pianist would play. I could 'hear' it through the week, and I would play it over and over in my mind.

"The choir director, Gerald Hines, took me on my first tour to San Francisco. Everyone started grabbing for this 'young pianist,' wanting me to play for them. I met Mahalia Jackson in that way, and she invited me to play piano on her recordings. Each time she came to California I was asked to play for her recording sessions."

It would take a whole book to tell about everything Albert Goodson did and the people with whom he associated—musicians such as Doris Akers, who wrote "Sweet, Sweet Spirit"; James Cleveland, popular recording artist; Thomas A. Dorsey, who wrote "Precious Lord, Take My Hand"; and the famed recording artist, Nat King Cole, just to name a few.

It seems that the most meaningful and lasting songs spring from a dark period in the life of the songwriter. Such was the case of Albert Goodson's famous song, "We've Come This Far by Faith."

"I was living in Chicago, alone," said Albert. "I was never married, and I didn't have a relative or a close friend in that city. People around me, with whom I was associating, were making large salaries and had much of this world's possessions, while I had very little and wasn't being paid properly. I became so discouraged that I seriously considered going back to Los Angeles.

"One day, during my depressed state, I sat down at the piano in a friend's home and began to play. A melody came to me that I liked, and so I continued to play it the rest of the day. As I played, the Lord seemed to speak to me saying, 'I have never failed you. You have come this far by faith.' Later, as I walked along the streets of Chicago I met a man who told me that he didn't believe in God, and yet, the words kept coming to me over and over again, 'You've come this far by faith.'

"I immediately knew that I had found words for my melody. I called Los Angeles and spoke to Thurston Frazier, a man with whom I was doing some music publishing. I told him that I had written a song called 'I've Come This Far by Faith.' After he heard it on the phone he said, 'Why don't you call it, "We've Come This Far by Faith"?' A leader of a large church in Chicago heard it, and that church sang it every Sunday for a full year. It seemed that people everywhere were singing my song. Thurston recorded it with Capital Records. It was put into a movie by Warner Brothers, for which they paid me $7,000."

Still, for a period of time, people tried to steal the rights to Goodson's songs, causing him to become so discouraged that he almost completely stopped writing. Who knows how many great songs might have issued from Goodson if it hadn't been for those unfortunate circumstances?

A song that is appreciated by a wide range of audiences is called a "crossover" song. And "We've Come This Far by Faith" has crossed over many lines, sung by soloists, small groups, and huge choirs. For many years it has been a favorite in the world of Southern Gospel Music.

Reflection

If we all could learn the lesson that God taught to Albert Goodson as He gave him his song, we, too, could learn to live victoriously. All along the way our greatest accomplishments have come by faith, and He has never failed to keep even one of His precious promises given to us in His Holy Word.

11

Born at Midnight

Where No One Stands Alone

Psalm 34:17–22

*The LORD is nigh unto them that are of a broken
heart; and saveth such as be of a contrite spirit.*

Someone asked, "Who is the most significant contributor of
Southern Gospel songs?" The answer came, "You mean other
than Mosie Lister?"

Mosie has been writing songs for God's people for more
than fifty years. He gave his heart and life to Christ at age
seventeen and soon thereafter began to write songs. He was
born in 1921, in the town of Cochran, Georgia, and grew up in
a very musical home, studying piano, violin, and guitar for several years.

In a recent interview he said, "I want to tell you something
that I have not previously shared in interviews like this. I grew
up on a farm. As a child I would walk around the fields and in
my mind I could hear choirs singing and orchestras playing. I
wanted so much to write songs that those choirs would sing
and the orchestras would play. I prayed, 'God, I'd like to be a
songwriter.' I prayed that prayer for a whole year."

God began to answer that prayer when Mosie was only eighteen years of age. He confessed, "I'm so amazed at what God has
allowed me to do. I thank Him and appreciate His blessings."

Along the way he took good advice from men like Adger M. Pace, who told him, "Be sure the tune can be whistled." And from Jake Hess who passed along these comments: "If you want your songs to live, write things that are eternally true, and people will not forget them."

After a tour of duty in the navy, Mosie formed a group called the Melody Masters. From that group he moved on to the legendary Statesmen as a singer, songwriter, and arranger.

One night in 1955 Mosie drove along a Georgia highway from Macon to Atlanta, a distance of about ninety miles. He was returning, alone, from a Southern Gospel concert, and it was about midnight.

"I heard the sound of the tires against the road. I wasn't really thinking of anything particular. All of a sudden I found myself singing. I started at the beginning of a little chorus and sang it all the way through. When I reached the end, I realized that I was singing something brand-new, yet something that I already knew. So I went back to the beginning and sang it again and again. It was almost as if I was singing along with someone else. I had the feeling that there was a choir and orchestra, and I was just a part, maybe a small part of something that was happening—something new and original. I really didn't know just what it was, and that was all that I had—just that chorus."

About a year later, Mosie remembered the chorus written on that lonely highway at midnight, and he struggled, searching for something to complete what he knew was a song. One evening he read Psalm 55, about David's spiritual and mental agony over his sin with Bathsheba and his having her husband killed. David searched for something to say to the Lord to show that he was sorry for those horrible sins. "I could tell that David felt so alone, so completely away from God—just totally alone. That idea suddenly gripped me, and I yelled to my wife, 'I'll be back in a minute.' I went out the front door and walked around the block. By the time I came back I had both verses in mind, and I quickly wrote them down. In the verses I tried to get inside David's turmoil and say something about how alone he felt, about how we can feel alone if we are far away from God."

In his song "Where No One Stands Alone," Mosie conveys the horror of loneliness. He uses a phrase much like the one in Scripture: Christ is hanging on the cross and cries out, "My God, why have You forsaken me?" Loneliness is a feeling of being estranged from the Lord, but how exhilarating to experience the joy of the Lord when we draw close to Him and realize that He is "holding" our hands.

Mosie has lived to hear great choirs and orchestras sing his songs. He has written hundreds of musical selections that have blessed the hearts of millions of God's people the world over, and have been recorded and performed by thousands of the famous, the near-famous, and the would-be-famous. He is one of the great choral arrangers of our time, having dozens of collections to his credit. For a number of years he has been under contract to Lillenas, one of our nation's leading Christian music publishers.

Today, Mosie lives in central Florida, keeping his long-time goal, "to write music that moves the heart and stirs the soul. I'm trying to do something in God's kingdom that will help someone and bring honor to God."

Reflection

If loneliness is your trial, then read the above Scriptures and the lyrics to Mosie's song, and thank God for His nearness and His presence.

12

Early One West Virginia Morning

Sweet Beulah Land

John 14:1–11

*And if I go and prepare a place for you, I will come
again, and receive you unto myself; that where I
am, there ye may be also.*

*O*ccasionally a single song brings acclaim and recognition to
its composer. Although the songwriter might have written scores
of songs, one seems to leap ahead of all of the others. Such was
the case with Squire Parsons and his most famous song, which
was named Song of the Year in 1981 by the Singing News Fan
Awards.

Parsons was born in Newton, West Virginia, in 1948 into the
home of Christian parents. His father was the song leader and
choir director of the local church, and sang with a gospel music group in a number of churches near Newton. The older
Parsons, in fact, figures prominently in the writing of his son's
song.

Squire gave his heart to the Lord at age nine at the Newton
Baptist Church and began his writing ventures eleven years
later. He studied music at a West Virginia college where he
majored in voice and bassoon. Although he played piano by
ear, he began to seriously study piano in college.

As a student he was for two years a bass soloist for Christ

United Methodist Church, in Charleston, West Virginia. He later said that it was a wonderful experience because he was exposed to the Christian classics, which influenced some of his later writing.

Upon graduation from college he was classified 1A with the military draft board and was soon to be inducted into the armed forces, but the principal at Hannan High School managed a deferment for him. Squire began teaching band and directed the choir at the school. His intention was to teach for one year, but he loved the people so much that he taught there for four years, at which time he joined the Kingsmen Quartet and began traveling with that Southern Gospel group.

When Squire was only nine, during a morning service in the small church in Newton where his father was song leader, the congregation was led in the old hymn, "Is Not This the Land of Beulah?" Squire reports that his dad's face seemed to glow as he led the song. The whole congregation seemed swept up in the wonderful prospect of the eternal land about which they were singing. The picture remained in the mind of young Parsons, and he remembers thinking, *Dad is looking into Beulah Land.*

He also reports, "One morning, years later, as I drove to my teaching job, my mind drifted back to that service in our little church. I was humming the old song as I topped one of the beautiful West Virginia mountains and faced a brilliant sun in all of its glory. All of a sudden, as I continued to think of that scene in our little church, I began to sing, but this time it was a different song, one I had never heard or sung before." It was the chorus to what has become his most widely known song, "Sweet Beulah Land."

Squire added, "I traveled on to the school. It was early and the students had not yet arrived. I wrote a verse to go with the chorus that had just been born. Five years went by before I wrote a second verse and recorded the song. That launched me into the ministry of a traveling gospel singer and songwriter."

Squire uses some very unusual phrases in the make-up of his song—phrases that are paradoxical in nature—such as being "homesick for a country to which I've never been." Yet faith is a key element in this highly descriptive song—the faith that we hold as we look toward heaven, faith that will "end in sight."

The name, "Beulah Land," is a long used term, but one that evokes happiness and sweetness in our hearts. The "longing for you" spoken of in the song expresses the hopes and feelings of Southern Gospel Music lovers.

Squire Parsons now crisscrosses our nation, singing his songs and reminding us of the beautiful prospect of "Sweet Beulah Land." He has written more than 800 songs, approximately 500 of which have been published or recorded. A book, *The Songs of Squire Parsons: The Millennial Collection,* was published in 2001, containing 280 of Parsons's songs.

Reflection

The anticipation of an eternal heavenly home makes our lives on earth all the more wonderful.

13

From Greek Philosophy to Southern Gospel

All Because of God's Amazing Grace

Ephesians 2:1–13

That in the ages to come he might show the exceeding riches of his grace in his kindness toward us through Christ Jesus.

Stephen Adams has made possibly the most extreme transition into Southern Gospel Music of any songwriter. Born into a Nazarene pastor's home in 1943, and a native of Woonsocket, Rhode Island, Stephen began his music training at age seven. How he came to take piano lessons is a story in itself.

Rita Rundlett was affiliated with the Boston Conservatory, and after the death of her husband, she moved near to a Nazarene college not far from the Adams home. Rita needed to earn money in order to support herself and her children.

"My Dad was a pastor and was going to college himself," said Stephen, "so he didn't have a lot of money for music lessons. He went to Mrs. Rundlett and asked, 'If I open up my house once a week as a studio and fill up your schedule, would you give my kids free music lessons?' She agreed to do so and began coming to the Adams home every Tuesday.

"After the piano lessons she would stay for supper and,

afterward, would go into the living room and play new songs that she had written. Dad was a tenor soloist and would sing her lovely songs.

"As a kid I was awestruck that someone's grief could be turned into something so positive. At the same time my dad was instilling into my brother and me a real love for literature and poetry. So the two were tied together for me.

"As a child, only eight years of age, the Lord spoke to my heart in a camp-meeting service, telling me that when I became older He wanted me to write music for the church to sing."

When Stephen was sixteen years of age, his dad accepted a call as pastor of a church in Frankfort, Indiana, only about forty-five miles from the home of Bill and Gloria Gaither. Someone in Frankfort suggested that he go to meet Gaither, a publisher of music in Alexandria. Stephen drove over to the Gaither home and, without an appointment, knocked on their front door. They opened their home to him—taking a real interest in this young, aspiring songwriter—inviting him to stay for supper.

Stephen was already a talented musician and the organist for his dad's church, so Gaither invited him to play organ accompaniment for the Gaither Trio in some of their church engagements.

Stephen was married after graduating from Indiana University with an undergraduate degree in Aristotelian (Greek) Philosophy and a graduate degree in English literature. God gave Stephen and his wife Janet two wonderful sons, Chris and Craig. During those years, in addition to teaching school, he traveled with such notable singers as Doug Oldham, the Gaither Trio, and Henry and Hazel Slaughter.

The mix of traveling and teaching school became too strenuous. Yet, in spite of his hectic schedule, he won an award as Young Educator of the Year. Following that honor he was selected by the education board to head the English department, and to go to Purdue University and pursue a doctorate. Stephen decided in favor of the music and left teaching to become a full-time keyboard artist and songwriter.

Following is Stephen's story behind one of his greatest songs.

"One Friday night, after getting out of class I drove up to New Haven, Indiana, for a concert with Doug Oldham, the Gaithers, and the Slaughters in a high school auditorium. I was to accompany Doug on the piano. I remember thinking on the way to the concert how much I was enjoying my career. The Lord was greatly blessing my wife, Janet, and me—we were new parents.

"Doug was first on the program. We did our set of songs and were to be followed by Henry and Hazel. I have always loved them very much. They were the kind of people I could look up to and admire in so many ways. As I walked off the stage, I stopped and sat down just behind the curtain. I wanted to hear their music.

"Henry turned to his wife during one of those special moments that we referred to as 'the quiet,' a time when the Lord was very close to us in the service. Henry, still sitting at the piano bench, took Hazel by the hand and began to speak of God's blessings. With tears in his eyes he said, 'You know, honey, everything we are and everything we hope to be is because of God's amazing grace at work in our lives.' I remember being struck by that thought, because God was being good to me. I was experiencing His grace at work in the life of my young family.

"I also remember how good it was to get back home after that busy weekend on the road. I taught school on Monday, and all through the day the thought of God's amazing grace kept rolling through my mind. I realized that I had the theme for a song. I left school, went right home, and sat down at our little spinet piano in the living room.

"After a short time I called my wife at her work and said, 'Is anyone listening to you?' She said, 'No.' I said, 'Good, because I'm going to sing to you.' I began to sing the song I had just written. It was a song that would mean a great deal to us in our early years.

The Speer Family found out about Stephen's song and recorded it. Since then it has been recorded by hundreds, if not thousands, of singers.

The first and second stanzas of Adams's song are a slight rewording of the first and fourth stanzas of John Newton's "Amazing Grace." The chorus is a joyous testimony of a Christian who anticipates a grand and "glorious morning" when we will see Jesus face to face—all because of His marvelous, amazing grace.

Reflection

Many words in Scripture are precious to us—"love," "peace," "forgiven," "happiness"—the list goes on. But no word in the Bible portrays the goodness of God more than does the word *grace*.

14

From Ridicule to a Reward

Each Step I Take

1 Peter 2:20–25

For even hereunto were ye called: because Christ
also suffered for us, leaving us an example, that ye
should follow his steps.

"Mother, that is a beautiful song. Let's write to America and get a copy." The young lad in the Philippine Islands in 1962 listened with his mother to the "Lutheran Hour." His mother had recently become a Christian and was being ridiculed by her husband and teenage son for her newfound faith in Christ. On this particular morning, a soloist on the radio program sang "Each Step I Take," an unusual song written by Elmo Mercer.

The letter was soon on its way to the United States, and after a considerable time, the musical composition arrived at their home. Having a copy of the song in hand made it even more precious to the boy. He and his father were both converted, in fact, as a result of having the song. The lad later went on to study in Manila for the gospel ministry.

As stated previously, the songs that are most lasting and meaningful—whether they be Southern Gospel songs, contemporary Christian songs, or traditional—are born of human suffering. Someone went through a dark period in his or her life and from that darkness came a ray of light, a sunbeam, a song.

"Each Step I Take" came during a discouraging period in the life of young Mercer. Although he had been writing music for five years at the time, this was to become his most famous song.

His first poetic efforts were the result of expressing exactly what he felt in his heart at the time. His mom and dad had brought him up in the church, which was greatly helpful in his music ministry.

Mercer has gone on to write more than one thousand songs, many of which have blessed the hearts of millions of people. His sincere desire is to serve Christ through sacred songs.

For many years Elmo was Chief Music Editor for the Benson Company, and during his music career he compiled and arranged many choral collections and octavo pieces for church choirs. A number of his books for piano and organ have enjoyed wide circulation.

What about *your* life? Is it totally and completely surrendered to Christ? Is your life counting for Him? Not everyone can write songs, but everyone can live a life of dedication to Christ. Everyone can live in a way that serves the Lord and brings honor and glory to God by following in Christ's footsteps and reflecting the words of Elmo Mercer's song.

Elmo's song has a message for each of us, namely, that we need not fear the unknown because Christ "goes before me." He leads us with a "loving hand," and we can hear His "whisper" along the way, His message of love to us. And in return we express our love to Him. Not only do we love Him, but we trust Him, "no matter come what may."

Reflection

God, in His infinite wisdom, does not allow us to see beyond today. In love, He has thrown a veil across our way so that we cannot see what lies ahead. Therefore, we must walk with Him each step of the way, trusting in Him and leaning on Him for every necessity of life. Can you say with Elmo Mercer, "Each step I take my Savior goes before me"?

15

From Suicide to Soulwinning

Room at the Cross for You

Proverbs 3:1–20

*Trust in the LORD with all thine heart; and lean
not unto thine own understanding. In all thy ways
acknowledge him, and he shall direct thy paths.*

$\mathcal{A}$ despondent young man, bent on taking his own life, walked
near a church where, inside, a service was being conducted by
Evangelist Willard Cantelon, with Al Garr directing the music
for the service. The troubled young man had a gun in his pocket
and was making his way toward a high bridge not too far from
the church. There, he intended to shoot himself near the edge
of the bridge, letting his body fall into the water.

As he passed the church, he heard Al Garr singing "Room at
the Cross for You." The young man was so gripped by its message that he made his way into the church, postponing his mission of horror. There he found Christ as his Savior and was
rescued from personal and spiritual disaster. "He later studied
for the ministry and became an evangelist. A motion picture
has been made of his life since that notable day when 'Room at
the Cross for You' pointed him to Christ," reported the late Ira
Stanphill, former pastor of the Rockwood Park Assembly of
God in Fort Worth, Texas, and composer of that song and
hundreds of others.

Because there is no such thing as luck or chance in the life of a Christian, it can only be concluded that God drew this young man to Him, although he chose a very unusual method to do so.

The story of the song's birth is also unique. Ira Stanphill was preaching in a series of revival services in Kansas City, Missouri. As was his custom, he asked the people to submit suggested song titles while the congregation sang. As the choir presented their favorite selections, he would write a gospel song, using as the title one of those submitted by the congregation.

On this particular Sunday morning, the people submitted about fifty ideas. Stanphill quickly thumbed through the titles and saw the words, "Room at the Cross for You." That title struck a responsive chord, and before the service was complete he had given to the world a memorable song.

Little did Stanphill realize at the time what an impact the song would have. He remembers that he thought the song would not, in fact, go far. He asked the people to come back that evening, promising that he would choose another one from the balance of titles and have an additional song ready. Although he spent much time choosing a title and was more cautious in forming the lyrics, the second song is not known at all. But "Room at the Cross for You" has been sung around the world.

Our lives are not lived by chance, but in either the permissive or directed will of God. Always watch for His direction in your life and accept as the handiwork of God those things that at the time seem unusual. Learn to say with Fanny Crosby, "His purposes will ripen fast, unfolding every hour. The bud may have a bitter taste, but sweet will be the flower."

We can be glad indeed that God directed Ira Stanphill to write "Room at the Cross for You." In the first verse he presents in poetic fashion the salvation plan that God has provided, not only for the young man told about in this story but for you and me. In the chorus, Stanphill thrice repeats the good news—"there's room at the cross for you." And not only you, but for all who come, though they be counted in the millions. And "though millions have come" God has made provision and there is always "room for one" more.

Reflection

Every day, before retiring, look back and recognize the hand of God as He quietly, tempestuously, strangely, or sometimes mysteriously moves to shape your life to make it more like His Son's. Trust Him to lead you toward the paths of righteousness.

16

From the Rapture to Christmas

More Than Wonderful

Isaiah 9:1–7

For unto us a child is born, unto us a son is given:
and the government shall be upon his shoulder:
and his name shall be called Wonderful,
Counsellor, The mighty God, The everlasting
Father, The Prince of Peace.

This is another unusual story from the prolific songwriting career of Lanny Wolfe, one of the most recognized names in the Southern Gospel genre of Christian music. Although highly educated and vastly experienced as a music professor, Wolfe's most notable work is his songwriting. Following is Wolfe's account of just how difficult it was for him to bring into being one of his most honored and blessed musicals.

"During the 1970s, in addition to songs I wrote for the many albums recorded by the trio, I also wrote my first two musicals, *Greater Is He That Is in Me* and *Noel, Jesus Is Born.* Because of the impact of the latter, my publisher at that time, the Benson Company, wanted me to do another musical. Although I had in mind doing a musical about the second coming of Christ, the decision makers at Benson thought that the marketplace wasn't ready for such a theme. They wanted me to write another Christmas cantata.

"In the process of the meetings, the president of the company suggested that I write a song for the musical based on Isaiah 9:6. I responded to the assignment and the song came easily.

"Our trio began using it, with great response from the audiences. I carried the song to the Benson Company and the response of Bob McKenzie, an official of the company was, 'You know, Lanny, I think you can write a better song. I don't think we should put that song into the musical.' I went away from the meeting discouraged. I know when an audience is responding to a song, and they responded greatly to 'More Than Wonderful,' which I had written for the cantata.

"At subsequent meetings, and after vigorous discussions with Bob McKenzie, I was allowed to put the song into the musical, although it was against his wishes. I also suggested that Larnelle Harris and Sandi Patti sing the song as a duet on the demonstration tape.

"'More Than Wonderful' won a Grammy Award for Larnelle and Sandi for their duet performance of it. The song was voted Song of the Year in 1984 by the Gospel Music Association, and I was honored as GMA's Songwriter of the Year. Although my songs had been nominated seven previous times, it was the first time that a song from a musical, rather than from an artist's project, had ever been chosen song of the year.

"I learned so much about God from this chapter in my life. First, if God gives you a 'child,' then nurture and protect it and don't let anyone destroy it. Second, when God wants to do something, He will do it in spite of everything or anyone who might stand in the way. Third, God sometimes uses people to disappoint us in order to accomplish what He wants to do in our lives. Sometimes what we call bad times are really blessings in disguise. God is always working for our good, even when we might not have a clue as to what He is doing."

In the lyrics to that song Lanny lists the promises of God—He will be the Counselor, the mighty God, the Prince of Peace, and the Father who will love us with a love that will not cease. In the next verse he proclaims that those promises are true and that God is "all that He promised to be." The chorus is one of the most descriptive and moving declarations about our Savior that has ever been penned.

Lanny Wolfe stood his ground and insisted that the song the Lord gave to him be put into the musical. In that way, it has been passed on to you and me.

Reflection

Not even a small fraction of His glory and His majesty can be imagined by mortals, who are finite. The infinite wonder of His person and His power defies our description.

17

From the Storm Comes a Song

Sheltered in the Arms of God

Psalm 61

*For thou hast been a shelter for me, and a strong
tower from the enemy. I will abide in thy tabernacle
for ever: I will trust in the covert of thy wings.*

The winds howled as Dottie Rambo walked along the beach
among the scattered pieces of driftwood. A small fire flickered
nearby. Once again, Dottie wanted to be alone to ponder the
thoughts that troubled her very soul. An unfaithful friend had
caused disappointment, and out of such troubled times a song
usually appeared. One was ever so near at that moment, stir-
ring in the heart of this lady who had been writing songs since
she was nine years old.

"There had been a very bad storm the day before," said Dottie,
"and the driftwood was scattered along the beach. I was going
through a time that was a low valley for me. It was sort of a
'storm' in my own life. As the white caps broke across the water, and as I walked among the driftwood and the seaweed with
my guitar strapped over my shoulder, I pondered the lyrics of
several songs that the Lord seemed to be giving to me at the
time.

"All of a sudden I thought, *Lord, this storm is so much like my
life, and yet, in the midst of the storms of life, You have been a shelter*

71

to me. When I can't take the storm, I run to You for that shelter and, suddenly, I feel secure.

"While thinking on those things and watching the storm as it kicked up the waters, I began to write a song. The melody was coming as I played my guitar, but I could not find an opening for the song. I could not find a way to interpret the song, something that would give it a springboard.

"As I continued to walk, I pled with the Lord, 'Lord, how am I going to start this song?' And, as I was talking to God, the closeness of the Lord touched me on the shoulder. I felt His presence, so real. I had a very warm feeling and these words came forth: 'Thank you, Lord, I feel the touch of your hand, so kind and tender.' Then I started to weep and I said, 'Lord, that is how I will open the song.'" The words kept coming and God gave Dottie a message for her own troubled heart. This message can also be for you and me. Why don't you sing it right now?

In the first verse Dottie describes how God often speaks to us in a very "kind and tender" fashion. As we hear this loving voice we are led to walk with Him, sensing His sheltering arms about us, driving away all fear.

As many songwriters have done, Dottie closes her song with a verse about heaven. She likens death to the call of God for His children—"come home my child," God says to us. And so we "fall asleep" on this earth and awaken in heaven, still "sheltered in the arms of God."

Perhaps there is a storm in your life. Maybe it brings heartache or fear. As you draw ever so close to the Lord Jesus through the reading of His Word, you, too, will find the touch of His hand "so kind and tender."

Reflection

There are days so dark that we desperately seek the face of our divine Friend. But even when darkness covers our world, He is there to guide by the touch of His hand and the light of His Word.

18

Goldie Encouraged Him

I'll Fly Away

Psalm 55:1–6

*And I said, Oh that I had wings like a dove! for
then would I fly away, and be at rest.*

The year was 1948, and the occasion was the funeral of my
grandfather, James Terry. In the small, rural Smyrna Baptist
Church, midway between Courtland and Moulton, Alabama, a
trio rose to sing a song that was literally sweeping the South.
The song was written just seventeen years before by one of our
nation's leading Southern Gospel songwriters, Albert E.
Brumley. It is one of more than six hundred songs that flowed
from his pen.

That song, "I'll Fly Away," has been played and sung in some
of the nation's largest auditoriums and presented by one of
our country's most popular symphony orchestras, the Boston
Pops. Chet Atkins was the guitar soloist for that recording. More
than a hundred of Brumley's songs have been recorded by countless singers for major music companies. He is the only gospel
songwriter to have four exclusive albums of his songs recorded
on major labels.

Albert Brumley's rural background made it natural for him
to appeal to the common man. Even as a small lad, picking
cotton in LeFlore County, Oklahoma, he knew he would much

rather be involved in music than in any other line of work. At age seventeen he began his serious music study, and in the next several years he received training and instruction from such notable men as Homer Rodeheaver, Virgil Stamps, and E. M. Bartlett, who wrote "Victory in Jesus."

In 1931, while teaching a singing school in Powell, Missouri, Brumley met, and later married, Goldie Edith Schell. He had already begun his songwriting, but had done nothing with the songs. Goldie encouraged him to send his songs to a publisher, assuring him that they were good and that "any publisher would be glad to publish them."

One of the first songs submitted was "I'll Fly Away." This song, written during the Depression, along with other Brumley songs, was carried to the nation by radio and traveling Southern Gospel quartets. People everywhere were receiving renewed hope as they listened to such songs as "Turn Your Radio On," "I'll Meet You in the Morning," "Jesus, Hold My Hand," and, of course, "I'll Fly Away."

It has often been said that Albert Brumley's songs have been used in more places and by more people than those of any other songwriter. His songs have been recorded by such well-known artists as the Chuck Wagon Gang, Red Foley, Jim Reeves, the Statesmen, the Blackwood Brothers, the Wills Family, Chet Atkins, Ernest Tubb, the Florida Boys, the Speer Family, Jimmy Dean, and Grandpa Jones, to name a few.

I am especially glad that he wrote "I'll Fly Away."

Reflection

"If I take the wings of the morning, . . . even there shall thy hand lead me, and thy right hand shall hold me" (Ps. 139:9–10).

19

He Looked like Colonel Sanders

It's Beginning to Rain

Acts 2:17–21

*It shall come to pass in the last days, saith God, I
will pour out of my Spirit upon all flesh: and your
sons and your daughters shall prophesy, and your
young men shall see visions, and your old men
shall dream dreams.*

A fireball of a Southern Baptist preacher came to Huntsville,
Alabama. J. Otis King preached in a tent revival, and thirteen-
year-old Aaron was among the listeners. The evangelist, with
white hair, a white goatee, dressed in a white suit with a string
bow tie, looked like Colonel Sanders but preached like Billy
Sunday. One night, after the sermon, Aaron hit the "sawdust
trail" and gave his heart to Jesus Christ.

So began the Christian journey of one of the great Southern
Gospel composers of all time. In 1950, Aaron Wilburn was
born to Eugene and Lola Wilburn in Ardmore, Alabama, near
the Tennessee line. He was one of seven children, most of whom
were active in their musical family group in their local Free
Will Baptist Church.

Aaron's first musical instrument was a guitar, bought and
paid for by himself with fourteen dollars he had made by picking cotton. He lamented the fact that it was a struggle for him

to pick as much as one hundred pounds in a single day while others picked up to three hundred pounds per day. What Aaron Wilburn lacked as a cotton picker he certainly makes up for as a singer and songwriter.

The Lord has allowed him to write in excess of eight hundred songs with more than six hundred of them recorded or published. At age sixteen he wrote "Modern Age of Progress," a song recorded by the famed Sego Brothers and Naomi. He's gone on from that beginning to influence the Southern Gospel genre of Christian music.

After spending several years as a musician with the Happy Goodman Family, and while enjoying tremendous success as a singer-songwriter, he attended the annual Quartet Convention one day in 1976.

"As I entered the hall with Aaron Brown, my publisher," said Wilburn, "the Cruise Family was on stage singing. I turned to Aaron and said, 'What a great line.' He asked, 'What line are you referring to?' I said, 'They're singing, "It's beginning to rain."' He turned to me and said, 'No, that isn't what they're singing; they're singing, "Let's begin to reign."' Even though I was mistaken, I still thought, *Wow! What a great title for a song!– 'It's Beginning to Rain!'*

"I began to quote the passage of Scripture in Joel where God says, 'I will pour out of my Spirit on all flesh: and your sons and your daughters shall prophesy.' He, listening to the song, almost ignored me. But I didn't mind because I was thinking of the great idea that had been given to me.

"I left before the concert was over and began driving toward Indianapolis, where I was to sing in a church during the Sunday morning and evening services. As I drove along I thought of the phrase, 'It's beginning to rain.' I placed a small tape recorder on the seat beside me into which I sang parts of a melody and some words, starting with 'It's beginning to rain . . .' I still have the cassette tape with all of the noise of passing cars and trucks, along with the singing and humming of my song ideas. I would lose the melody from time to time, but it all ended up with 'It's beginning to rain.'

"The day after the Sunday church services in Indianapolis, I drove to the home of Bill and Gloria Gaither in Alexandria, Indiana. We had scheduled a morning writing session, and I arrived around ten o'clock in the morning. Gloria had baked a batch of cookies, so we visited for a while, drinking coffee and eating cookies.

"We then moved to the living room where I slid onto the piano bench, because Bill had asked me to sing some of my old country songs that he enjoyed. After I sang a few songs, Bill asked, 'Do you have any good ideas?' I said, 'Well, I have this one,' and I showed them what I had done with 'It's Beginning to Rain.' Bill replied, 'That's the song we need to write!'

"We started writing and had a great time together as we threw lyric lines back and forth to each other. Bill took the melody that I had started and filled in around it, making it what it is today. Gloria is such a great lyricist. She is phenomenal. She took the ideas and the Scripture that I had shared and sat over to one side writing some wonderful lyrics. It all came together so well and so quickly. We had the whole song finished by noon.

"We sat around for a while and sang our song. I remember that Bill was so moved he had to occasionally wipe the tears away. Gloria said, 'We've written a special song today.'

"I began to sing it in some of the conferences and churches. Doug Oldham was the first to record it, followed by the Gaither Trio, Ken Copeland, and a number of others. It has now become more of a 'pew song' and has been used a great deal on television. It is also being included in collections for choirs."

Aaron, Bill, and Gloria have masterfully blended a beautiful melody with God's creation—turtle doves, trees, silent clouds—and the visions and dreams of the young and the old, to make for you and me a lilting song of joy and promise. The "whosoever will" invitation in the chorus—to participate in God's wonderful provision—is rapturous, indeed.

Reflection

My favorite part of this song is in the second verse where the young and the old are brought together as they share their visions and dreams—and "reach for each other."

20

He Sang for His Own Funeral

We Shall See Jesus

1 John 3:1–3

*Beloved, now are we the sons of God, and it doth
not yet appear what we shall be: but we know that,
when he shall appear, we shall be like him; for we
shall see him as he is.*

If Dianne Wilkinson cut her finger she would bleed Southern Gospel Music. "It is very dear to my heart," she told me. She also loves her church, Springhill Baptist Church, in Dyersburg, Tennessee, pastored by her brother, James Branscum. She is the church pianist and teacher of the Open Door Sunday School Class. The people of the church know of her success as a songwriter, but they relate to her as part of their church family. "I have always had a music ministry in my church," she said, "and that is where my calling is." Her loyalty and love for her local church is inspiring.

She was born Dianne Branscum in Blytheville, Arkansas, a small town in the northeast part of the state, just across the Mississippi River from her present residence. As a small child she was often carried by her mother, Blanche, and her mother's sister, Mavis, to the Ellis Auditorium in nearby Memphis, Tennessee, to hear the Blackwood Brothers, the Statemen, the Speer Family, the LeFevres, and other well-known Southern Gospel singers of that era.

In her early twenties Dianne felt the Lord nudging her to become a serious student of the Bible. She purchased commentaries and study materials that would help her to learn and understand what God is saying to us in His Word. She now believes that the Lord led her in that direction because He wanted her songwriting to be true to the Word of God.

During the next twenty years she wrote nearly three hundred songs, some of which have become standards in the genre of Southern Gospel music. The Cathedrals recorded sixteen songs written by Dianne, and one of them is the subject of this story.

In an interview Dianne said, "When you are writing for the Cathedrals and you love quartet music like I do, so much of it comes out just straight ahead, quartet to the bone. And that is really what I'm doing these days. Traditional quartets are more popular then ever, and they're always looking for new songs that sound old."

Dianne relates how she came to write "We Shall See Jesus."

"I never plan to write a song. I cannot write songs on demand. I never could do that—wish I could.

"I was living in West Memphis, Arkansas, in 1981, and I began to think about the times when Jesus was on a hillside with people gathered around Him. As I thought of that setting, I wondered what it must have been like to just reach out and touch His hand—to be there in His presence, face to face. Suddenly, I realized that one day we will have the same opportunity that those people in Bible days had. Some day I will see Him just as they saw Him, as they sat with Him on the hillside, as He fed the thousands, touched the blind eyes, and healed the broken spirits. The song began to unfold in that way—in a triple setting."

In the song Dianne describes two other occasions when Jesus was on a hillside—once when He was being crucified to pay our sin debt, and the other after His resurrection when He blessed His disciples and then rose to the heavens, promising "to come back again."

The chorus is sung only once, after the trilogy of scenes where Christ is described. It rises in a triumphant crescendo as we are reminded of the second coming of our Lord, when He will return in glory and power. Then . . . "we shall see Jesus, just as He is."

One day Roger Bennett, twenty years pianist for the Cathedrals, called Dianne and said that they were going to put her song on a project called "Live in Atlanta," and that they had a front row seat reserved for her. This was the first time the song was to be sung in public. As Glenn Payne beautifully sang the three verses there was almost a stunned silence, but as he moved into the triumphant chorus singing, "We shall see Jesus, just as they saw Him," the audience came to its feet. After that, wherever they sang the song, the audience reaction was the same.

The Cathedrals kept that song in their program until Payne's death. "It became Glenn's signature song," said Wilkinson. In fact, when they had Glenn Payne's celebration of fifty years in Southern Gospel Music, Dianne was invited and presented to him the pages of a pad, beautifully framed, on which were scrawled the lyrics to "We Shall See Jesus." The gift was the actual pages on which she'd written the lyrics for the first time. She added, "Some time later, I sat at his funeral and watched them play the video of Glenn singing that song—at his own memorial service."

Reflection

We have all often wondered just how Jesus looked while here on this earth and how He looks today. The Bible says that when we get to heaven we shall know as we are known. Yes, we shall see our wonderful Lord, "just as He is."

21

His Own Song Led Him to Christ

Ten Thousand Angels

Matthew 26:47–66

*Thinkest thou that I cannot now pray to my Father,
and he shall presently give me more than twelve
legions of angels?*

*R*arely in the history of hymnology has a composer been led
to Christ by his own song. Such was the case with Ray Overholt.
God literally picked him up out of the darkness and confusion
of the nightclubs and brought him under His loving care, using
Ray's own song in an unusual manner.

Ray Overholt was born in Middleville, Ohio, in 1924. He
seemed destined to a career in music from age eleven when his
dad gave him his first guitar. He rose to a measure of success,
hosting his own television show and appearing on Kate Smith's
national program.

In 1958, then thirty-six years of age and at the height of his
show-business career, Ray Overholt wrote his now-famous song,
"Ten Thousand Angels." Following is his story as he related it
to me.

"I had left my television show, 'Ray's Roundup' and entered
the nightclub circuit. I was drinking pretty heavily at this time.
I began thinking that there must be a better life than the nightclub, show-business whirlwind. I was so intent on changing my

lifestyle that I went home and told my wife that I was quitting all of the smoking, drinking, and cursing. I wanted to clean up my own life. Why I was doing all of this I didn't know, but I knew there were people praying for me.

"One day I thought, *I've written secular songs, but I'd like to write a song about Christ.* I opened the Bible, which I knew very little about, and began to read the portion of Scripture that describes Jesus in the Garden of Gethsemane telling Peter to put away his sword. I read where Jesus told Peter that he could ask His Father and He would send twelve legions of angels. I didn't know at the time that that would have been more than 72,000 angels.

"I thought a good title for a song would be 'He Could Have Called Ten Thousand Angels.' I didn't know what had happened during the life of Christ, so I began doing a little research. The more I read about Jesus, the more I admired Him for what He had done. I then remembered that He did this all for me, also.

"I was playing in a nightclub in Battle Creek, Michigan, when the Lord impressed me to write the song. I wrote the first verse and put it in my guitar case. I then gave the club my notice that I was quitting. As I opened my guitar case to put my instrument away, one of the other musicians saw the music written out and he asked, 'What are you doing there?' I told him I was writing a song about Jesus. He asked the title and I told him. He said, 'It will never go.' I asked, 'Why not?' He said, 'I don't even like the title.' But I finished the song and sent it to a publishing house, which reluctantly agreed to publish it.

"Sometime later I found myself singing at a small church. I sang 'He Could Have Called Ten Thousand Angels.' Following my singing, a preacher gave a message that gripped my heart. I knew I needed Christ, so I knelt there and accepted, as my Savior, the One whom I had been singing and writing about."

Ray Overholt became a traveling singer and preacher. He has written a number of other songs, but none so moving as "Ten Thousand Angels."

Because Ray was not a Christian at the time, he did not realize the horror that he was to describe in his song. No death has ever been more excruciatingly painful than crucifixion—and the Romans mastered it. By design, death on a cross was not quick. No vital organs were damaged, so it was a slow, agonizing demise. Soldiers would first whip the victim with a scourge and then force him to carry his own crossbeam to the execution site. Once suspended on a cross, the hours in a strained position took its toll on the individual's body, causing difficulty in breathing—and often suffocation. Some victims died of heart failure. And sometimes a person would hang alive for days, finally succumbing to death as welcome relief.

Thousands of men were crucified over nearly a thousand years. Crucifixion ended in A.D. 337 when Constantine the Great, out of respect for the Son of God and His crucifixion for the whole world, banned this hideous practice forever.

In the lyrics Overholt describes the crucifixion and the suffering that led up to the event that looms larger than life to you and me. His whole theme is the willingness of Jesus to endure, alone, the inhuman ordeal of crucifixion, never once giving thought to calling for the help of the Father or "ten thousand" angels who would come at His beckoning. Overholt says, "He died alone, for you and me."

Reflection

Before we knew Him, God loved us. And so He drew us to Him through His Son and set us free.

22

Hitchhiking Through the Night

Without Him (I Could Do Nothing)

John 15:1–14

*I am the vine, ye are the branches: He that abideth
in me, and I in him, the same bringeth forth much
fruit: for without me ye can do nothing.*

$\mathcal{M}$ylon LeFevre has had a most unusual life as a soldier, a
songwriter, a singer, and a gospel preacher. He was born in
Gulfport, Mississippi, in 1944, and was one of five children
born to Gospel Music Hall of Fame members Urias and Eva
Mae LeFevre. He said of his early years, "Everyone in my family
played musical instruments, which lay all about the house. I
learned to play them as soon as my hands were large enough,
starting with the ukulele and the mandolin. As I grew older I
learned to play the guitar and the bass."

Mylon's two brothers and one of his sisters, who were several years older than he, sang with their parents as a family
group called "The LeFevres." In addition, his brothers and one
sister sang on many occasions as a touring group. He reported,
"As a small child my parents stood me on the end of a piano
bench to sing my first song in church. When you were a LeFevre
you sang about Jesus whether you liked it or not. My parents
were in church every time the doors were opened. When I was
about twelve or thirteen years of age I gave my sins and my

problems to Jesus, but I didn't give Him my life. That did not happen until 1980 when I was thirty-five years of age.

"As a high school senior I had no desire to join the army, but because the draft was enforced at the time, I deemed it more desirable to volunteer for six months active duty than to be drafted and have to serve for two years. I wanted to get the head shaving thing over with because I intended to grow about two or three feet of hair. I wanted to get on with my life, so fourteen days after graduation I was gone.

"Although I knew very little about music, other than the playing of the instruments by ear, I began to write songs while still in high school. I wrote a song that I thought was quite good, and I played and sang it for one of my heroes, a very dear friend of our family, J. D. Sumner—also a Gospel Music Hall of Fame member. His response was, 'Son, that's not a complete song. You need verses as well as the chorus you have written.' And so I wrote two verses to complete the song. My Uncle Alf, an excellent musician, put the song in manuscript form, and I titled it "Without Him."

"While in the army, stationed at Fort Jackson, South Carolina, I received a phone call from my mother who wanted me to come to Memphis, Tennessee, to a quartet convention where she and my dad were scheduled to sing. She wanted me to sing my song that she loved. After taking extreme measures, I secured a three-day pass from my sergeant and hit the highway—hitchhiking.

"After hitching rides with truckers all through the night and the next day—a distance of five hundred miles—and after being rained on several times, because I walked constantly between rides, I arrived at the convention hall just fifteen minutes before my parents were to go on stage. I was dirty, unshaven, and still had my green army uniform on, but my mother introduced me and onto the stage I walked, shaved head and all.

"My mom said, 'My son has written a song, and I want you to hear it.' Little did I know it at the time, but my song was being recorded by Felton Jarvis, a producer for Elvis Presley. They had built a small 'booth'—recording studio—for Elvis just off stage with a one-way mirror. He and his fiancée, Pricilla, were sitting in the booth at the time, watching my performance and hearing the song. Elvis, whose response was very favorable, invited me to join them in the booth. He recorded my song later that same week, and it was put onto one of his religious projects, 'How Great Thou Art,' which became his biggest selling album. By the end of the year 'Without Him,' as well as other songs I had written, had been recorded by a hundred and twenty-six artists."

In the lyrics LeFevre describes the plight of a man who might try with his own works or his own merit to gain favor with God. In the opening line of the first verse the theme of the song is emphasized. The balance of the lyrics admits that "without Him" we would surely fail, be drifting, dying, enslaved, and hopelessly lost. He closes with a victorious line of thanksgiving that expresses "with Jesus" we are saved.

Today this song, based on John 15:15, is a standard on the Southern Gospel Music scene, and has appeared in choral arrangements and on countless recordings. Another influential factor in the song's popularity is that since 1963 it has been included in virtually all major hymnals.

Mylon LeFevre continues to write songs, having written 500 to 600 to date, with approximately 110 of them recorded. He has been involved in the recording of 49 albums and CDs, and has won Grammy Awards and Dove Awards, as well as Song of the Year Awards. Eighteen of his songs have risen to number one on the music charts.

Mylon and his wife, Christi, have one daughter, Summer. They make their home in Ft. Worth, Texas. Summer is the wife of Peter Furler, founding member of the contemporary Christian group, News Boys. When the Lord called Mylon to preach, he had a Christian contemporary music band, "Mylon and Broken Heart." Through the following years the group saw more than 200,000 young people come to know Christ in their concerts and services.

Mylon LeFevre continues to preach the Word of God in churches across America, and sings some praise and worship at each service.

Reflection

My strength—and yours—is much too weak when confronting the trials of life or even the everyday chores. We can be victorious only when we realize that our abilities and our power emanate from Christ. We can accomplish every task if we do them through Christ and depend on Him for strength (see Phil. 4:13).

23

Human Struggle Inspires a Song

Learning to Lean

2 Corinthians 12:7–10

*And he said unto me, My grace is sufficient for
thee: for my strength is made perfect in weakness.*

ohn Stallings was only sixteen years of age when he began
his songwriting career. A self-taught musician who travels as a
singing evangelist, John has had 50 of his more than 180 songs
published. His songs have been recorded and sung by such
notables as Bill Gaither, Kenneth Copeland, George Beverly
Shea, the Billy Graham Crusade Choir, and Jeannie C. Riley,
just to name a few. Scores of Southern Gospel singing groups
have recorded or used his songs, a remarkable achievement
for this Georgia native from the small town of Griffin, near
Atlanta.

At age thirty-four, while pastoring a church in Montgomery,
Alabama, Stallings's serene little world began to tumble around
him. One of his three daughters nearly died with a serious
illness and another was almost killed in an automobile accident. During this time, he felt the need to resign from his Alabama pastorate, and he moved to Florida. His furniture had to
be stored in three different places while Stallings tried to con-
struct a home, but things were not going well. For years he'd
been preaching about living by faith—now he would have to

learn to do so. In the midst of all these struggles, a song title began rolling around in his mind.

One day he sat down in the living room of the place where he lived at the time and wrote the now-familiar chorus to his famed song, "Learning to Lean." The chorus was an expression of his heart—a testimony of learning to depend upon God—the only One who has the power to give strength to overcome any and all difficulties, more power than Stallings ever dreamed possible. The song is written in the present tense, indicating that the singer is still learning every day.

Stallings sang the chorus in some of his services as an "altar service" song. Much to his surprise, while in a church in Cape Girardeau, Missouri, the pastor, after hearing the chorus, published it in his church bulletin. People began to sing the chorus and to ask about it.

After writing the chorus, Stallings thought very little about it because, in his words, "It came so easily." Now, he thought, *Well, if they like the chorus so much, then I'll try to write some verses to go with it.* And he did so about six or eight months following the writing of the chorus. That was in 1975, and the rest is history. The song swept the country and has been a favorite since.

Stallings tells of one lady who was so bent on destroying herself that she actually held a gun to her head. Suddenly from another room she heard the strains of "Learning to Lean." She put the gun aside and now credits this song with saving her from suicide.

A man who is now pastoring a church in Louisiana became a Christian because he heard a traveling musical group sing the song. And a number of pastors have testified that the hearing of that song helped them through low valleys in their ministries, causing them to keep on for the Lord. It is the only song that has ever won all three of the major sacred-song awards in the same year (1977): the Dove Award, the Singing News Award, and the Quartet Convention Award.

Blessings on John Stallings, for allowing the Lord to use him in giving "Learning to Lean" to all of us. The "joy I can't explain," the "glorious victory each day," and the "peace so serene" spoken of in the verses are a message from God and have had an impact on those who love the song.

Reflection

When we have come to the end of our endurance, the Lord's strength in us has only begun. To be empowered in the midst of weakness, we need only lean on Him.

24

I Didn't Write the Song

What a Day That Will Be

Revelation 21:1-7

*And God shall wipe away all tears from their eyes;
and there shall be no more death, neither sorrow,
nor crying, neither shall there be any more pain: for
the former things are passed away.*

*F*rank and Margaret Hill were somewhat prophetic when they named their son James Vaughn Hill. They selected the name from a convention song book published by James D. Vaughn, one of the pioneers of the Southern Gospel genre of Christian music. Jim Hill grew up to have a long and colorful career in Southern Gospel Music.

Jim was converted in 1946 at a Baptist camp meeting in Wheelersburg, Ohio, along with three of his friends. They formed the Camp Meeting Boys trio, affording Jim his first experiences with singing before a congregation.

As a young man he was a voice student of Mildred Deering, a graduate of the Cincinnati Conservatory of Music. She urged him to attend her alma mater, considering his voice to be of Metropolitan caliber. Instead, he obtained a degree in business administration from Ohio Business College and afterward studied at Ohio University for two years. He then turned his face toward Southern Gospel Music and never looked back.

After his discharge from the army in 1954, he formed the Golden Keys Quartet. Some time later Danny Gaither joined the group and was very instrumental in their success. Promoted by Lloyd Orrell, they began to sing with many of the leading quartets of that era, even appearing at the National Quartet Convention. They were often asked by the pros, "Where are you getting all of your music?" Jim told them, "Danny's brother, Bill Gaither, is writing for us." Jim says, "I laugh now as I remember their question, 'Who is Bill Gaither?'"

In 1962, Jim joined the Stamps Quartet—his first professional venture into Southern Gospel Music—who represented the Stamps Music Company. As manager of the quartet, Jim had the opportunity to work with and encourage such young singers as Terry Blackwood, Mylon LeFevre, Roger McDuff, and John Hall.

A dream came true for Hill when, in 1968, he was asked to sing in the famed Statemen Quartet from Atlanta, Georgia. Jim says, "I'm thankful to have had the opportunity to sing with one of the greatest tenors in gospel music, the late Rosie Roselle. The Statemen were my idols, and I never realized that some day I would be walking on stage with them. I can truly say, 'I am blessed.'"

Although Jim considers that his most rewarding accomplishment came through his writing songs that have touched the lives of millions, one of the greatest blessings—one that reached the innermost recesses of his own heart—came in a Baptist church years ago. It was much like a singing convention. A little girl, cute as a doll, from an orphanage and wearing a homemade dress, walked to the platform and began singing, "There is coming a day when no heartache shall come . . ." and on and on until she finished the song, "What a Day That Will Be." Jim said, "It touched my heart to no end!"

Many years later, that line "What a Day That Will Be" became a song title. But Jim declares that he didn't actually write the song. He says that God wrote the song and just "handed me the pen" to put it on paper. The following information is extracted from copies of articles that appeared in *Singing News Magazine;* "Angels on Earth," a Guideposts Publication; and the Huntington, West Virginia *Herald Dispatch,* all sent to me by Hill.

The song came through the affliction of his mother-in-law, Mrs. Stella Baldridge, the wife of Baptist evangelist Al Baldridge. At age fifty she suffered a stroke that rendered her paralyzed. All through her marriage, she had kept the home fires burning, raising three children and trying to be supportive of her itinerant husband, who had dedicated his whole life to God by faith. Hill said, "I could not understand this; I became very concerned."

On one occasion Hill, his wife, and his wife's sister drove to see Mrs. Baldridge, who was in need of constant care. As they motored along Jim began to sing. He sang words that had been dropped into his heart several days before while sitting on the back porch steps looking into the sky, thinking about his mother-in-law. After Jim had finished singing, they sang the song again with the ladies adding the harmony.

When they reached the Baldridge home something wonderful happened. They sang their new song for their "beloved patient," and for the first time in three years she smiled and showed signs of excitement. Jim said, "I knew then that there was more in that song than Jim Hill could write. It did not come from me." He immediately knew the purpose for his receiving of the song from the Lord.

Jim and the quartet began to sing it, much to the delight of their congregations. It was soon recorded and published. Since that time more than one thousand singing groups and individuals have recorded, "What a Day That Will Be"! It was the first song he wrote, and it has become now a "standard" in Southern Gospel Music. It also appears in many church hymnals and has been translated into several other languages.

Jim and his wife, Ruth, make their home in Middletown,

Ohio, where they attend the Town Boulevard Church of God. They have one daughter, Susan Webster, and two grandchildren. The Gaither Homecoming videos, on which he often appears, have given Hill so much exposure, he is once again doing concerts.

Reflection

Far beyond anything you and I can imagine will be the joys of heaven. We cannot, with our finite minds, go into that level of bliss. We trust God with the future, and all of us who know Christ look forward to the joys that will one day be shared— around His throne.

25

It All Started at Shoney's

When He Was on the Cross (I Was on His Mind)

Romans 5:6–9

But God commendeth his love toward us, in that,
while we were yet sinners, Christ died for us.

*W*hen Mike Payne was a senior in high school, he wanted to be involved with a music group. So he set out to make it happen. First, he bought a guitar and some music books. Then he read the book, took a few lessons, and learned to play. He then bought a set of drums and a bass guitar and taught two of his brothers, Mark and Keith, to play them. Thus, in 1971, the Mike Payne Trio was born. As time went by and other people joined the group, they changed the name to the Glorious Gospel Heirs. In 1990, Mike was called of the Lord to preach, and the group developed into a different trio, the Paynes, consisting of Mike, his wife Loreen, and their daughter Sandra.

Mike was born in 1953 to Thurman and Carmia Payne in Iaeger, West Virginia. He became a Christian at an early age and loves to share the testimony concerning his conversion experience.

"I became a Christian when I was twelve years old in a little store-front Missionary Baptist Church in Cleveland, Ohio. One night during a revival the preacher was saying, 'You need Jesus.' I looked at my dad and said, 'That preacher says that I need

Jesus.' My dad said, 'Well, you're too young to really under-stand all of that.' The evangelist continued to preach, and I waited a few more minutes and said, 'Dad, I may be too young to understand it, but I think Jesus wants to know me, and I definitely want to know Him—and I need Him.' I slipped out of the pew and went toward the altar, and as I looked around I saw that my dad had also come to the altar to be saved." Memo-ries of that night are very special to Mike and his dad.

Mike's first efforts at songwriting were simply to change the lyrics of popular, secular tunes. In places where the Mike Payne Trio appeared they sang songs like "I Can't Stop Loving You," simply changing the lyrics to reflect a Christian message. Mike later met a songwriter who composed his own tunes and he thought, *Wait a minute, if he can do that, I can do it, also.* That led to an incredible career of writing one favorite Southern Gos-pel song after another. His "Angels Step Back" was the most played of all Southern Gospel songs in 1986.

Mike related a most unusual story concerning another of his very popular songs.

"In 1983, our group was to release an album titled, 'I'm a Jesus Fan.' I was searching for a particular song, a slow ballad—I wanted to have a variety of songs on the project. I had thrown around many ideas, but nothing at all seemed to click.

"The night before we were to record, my wife, Loreen, and I were in a Shoney's restaurant and happened to see Ronny Hinson, along with a number of his friends and business asso-ciates. I mentioned to him that we were to go to a studio the following day to record a new album, and that I needed an-other song. He asked, 'What are you working on?' I said, 'Well, I have an idea about the theme for a song—"when He was on the cross He was thinking about me."'

"As Ronny was giving thought to that phrase, I continued, 'What I want to say in the song is, "When Jesus was on the cross, He saw those standing around Him, with their need, but He also looked into the future and saw me, and was thinking about me and my need."' Ronny said, 'Instead of saying, "When He was on the cross He was thinking about me," why don't you say, "When He was on the cross, I was on His mind."' I said, 'Oh boy, that sounds great!' Ronny jokingly said to me, 'I'm going home and write about that.' And I said, 'Oh no, you're not!'

"We got together that night in my hotel room. While Loreen was trying to sleep—of course, she couldn't sleep—Ronny and I were quietly writing a song that Loreen was to record the next day. Through the night we quietly exchanged ideas about the lyrics and softly hummed bits of the melody to each other. When the morning came we had finished our song. We both had expressed what was in our hearts and minds at the time. We had lyrics written down, but no melody on paper, only in our minds.

"We sang it to Loreen and asked, 'What do you think?' She said, 'I like it, I really do!' That same morning we went to the Hilltop Studios in a suburb of Nashville and recorded 'When He Was on the Cross, I Was on His Mind,' which was then included on the new album.

"Ronny Hinson was present in the studio when it was being recorded and decided straight away that he would 'pitch' 'When He Was on the Cross, I Was on His Mind' to the Florida Boys. He did so and unabashedly told them, 'This is your "number one" song and it will be the "song of the year."' Although the song helped the Payne family's album 'I'm a Jesus Fan' to be a very profitable project, it went to greater heights as the predictions Ronny made to the Florida Boys came true. 'When He Was on the Cross' became the number one song on all of the major Southern Gospel charts, and was Song of the Year in 1985 and 1986. It was the first time I ever cowrote a song, but it was a unique experience." Payne later reported that, "Writing with Ronny was truly a dream come true."

In the song, as the angry mob circle the cross of Christ, reviling Him and casting their ridicule in His face, He was, in

His infinite power and wisdom, able to turn His thoughts toward the need of His accusers and toward us who would come much later.

Many unusual stories could be told about Mike Payne's experiences with this Southern Gospel "classic." He reported to me that, to date, he has written more than 280 songs with approximately 80 percent of them being recorded or published. He would be the first to give Christ all of the glory and praise for His goodness in allowing him to touch the lives of millions of people through his music.

Reflection

It could not be more humbling to you and me than to realize that when Jesus was enduring the most horrible death ever devised by sinful man—crucifixion—He was providing a way of salvation for us. For nearly one thousand years men were crucified, but none—save Jesus Christ our Lord—were able to make the cross a badge of honor. He truly looked down through the corridors of time and saw me—and you—and provided for our great need.

26

It Started by the Creek Bank

We Shall Behold Him

Revelation 1:1–7

*Behold, he cometh with clouds; and every eye shall
see him, and they also which pierced him: and all
kindreds of the earth shall wail because of him.
Even so, Amen.*

The small rural town of Madisonville, Kentucky, gave to the world one of the all-time great gospel songwriters, Dottie Rambo. Songs that are meaningful to Christians everywhere flow from her pen, and the list of favorites is long, indeed.

It all started when Dottie was only eight years of age. She came home one day and began to quote a poem to her mother, who was cooking in the kitchen. She had just written it down by the creek bank. Her mother began to weep with joy as she realized that her little girl, one of her eleven children, had a wonderful gift from the Lord. At age eleven Dottie wrote a song that was sung by the Happy Goodman Family and recorded by Governor Jimmy Davis of Louisiana.

During the following years God gave Dottie hundreds of marvelous songs, which are still being sung by people around the world. Heartaches and disappointments were scattered among her triumphs, yet out of those periods of hurting, God gave to her some of her most blessed songs.

In 1981, Dottie reached what seemed to be the zenith of her writing career. At that time she was singing in a tent revival in Ohio. About sunset, she and a young lady who was singing with her drove to the large tent from their motel.

"I looked up," Dottie related to me, "and saw one of the most beautiful and unusual cloud formations. I have always loved beautiful cloud formations and have often been fascinated when I saw a formation that resembled a person or an object. I sensed as I watched that the Lord was about to give me something wonderful for the church. I saw colors that I had never seen in my lifetime. It seemed that the clouds almost took on the form of angels. The colors were so brilliant and unusual—blues, azures, and amber.

"Presently the clouds parted and there seemed to be a straight passageway through the formation. By this time I was weeping so much that I couldn't see to drive. It seemed, as the clouds parted, as if I could see the Savior coming in the clouds with trumpets sounding.

"I said to my young friend, 'Patty, you're going to have to drive. I can no longer see.' We changed places and continued to drive. Patty asked, 'What's wrong? Are you sick?' She didn't know that the Lord was giving me a song. It was being written in my heart because I had nothing on which to write.

"I then said, 'Patty, would you like to hear what the Lord just gave to me?' I began to sing my song. Soon she was weeping and had to pull the car to the side of the road. We were a little late to church that night, but before we reached the tent the Lord had given me the whole song. When I got there I could play the entire piece on my guitar. Every phrase was exactly as it should be. Changes were not necessary. It just came like a well-spring."

Dottie's description of the unfolding of the sky and the "thunders of praise" are vintage Rambo expressions. The second verse builds from the "shout of His coming" to the rising of those who sleep from their "slumbering place," to the changing in a moment of those who remain alive. The repeated phrase in the chorus, "We shall behold Him," crescendos with a beautiful melody, creating a sense of majesty.

Sandi Patti recorded "We Shall Behold Him" and helped make the song known in almost every nook and cranny of our nation. Because of this song, Sandi Patti was named Vocalist of the Year in 1981. In that same year, Dottie Rambo received Dove awards as Songwriter of the Year and the song itself was named Song of the Year.

Thank you, Dottie Rambo, for giving to the world this marvelous Christian song.

Reflection

The Lord's coming is the beginning of an eternity of joy for every Christian. What a marvelous day when we behold the Savior—face to face, in all of His glory.

27

Joy for the Taking

Happiness Is the Lord

Psalm 144:9–15

Happy is that people, whose God is the LORD.

$\mathscr{I}$ra F. Stanphill was born in Belview, New Mexico, in 1914. He has written more than 550 songs, the most popular of which are "Mansion over the Hilltop," "Room at the Cross," and, of course, "Happiness Is the Lord."

His songwriting on many occasions took place in unusual places, but one of his methods involved the people of a church congregation. He would, at the beginning of a service, ask the people to hand in phrases that they thought would be good titles for Christian songs. During the service, while others were speaking or singing, he would write a song, using one of the titles submitted by the congregation. He would then sing the song before the service was dismissed.

On many occasions, the Lord gives a songwriter a song when he or she least expects it. Such was the case with Ira Stanphill one afternoon in 1974, in Fort Worth, Texas.

As he drove home from his church office, the car radio was tuned to a commercial station. Some programs were sponsored by establishments that advertised their "happy hour" and their alcoholic beverages, and cigarettes were advertised in terms of how they bring happiness. The word *happiness* was used several times in the ads. Ira related to me that he thought at the time, "Happiness does not come with these things, but with knowing Christ." He continued, "As this thought really took over my mind I began to sing. I sang a new song, composing words and melody as I drove along. I sang it almost as it is published today."

"As I reached home, I ran in with a broad smile. My wife asked, 'What's the good news?' My answer was, 'Well, I just got a song.' 'Let's hear it,' she said. I told her that I didn't have it down yet, and so I went straight to the piano. In about fifteen to twenty minutes I had the finished work.

"I taught it to the people of my church. They picked it up quickly and sang it enthusiastically. So I mailed it to the Zondervan Corporation, the company for which I was writing at the time. They published it right away in several forms."

"Happiness Is the Lord" made its way across the United States and into other countries. Many hymnals today contain this infectious song written by a pastor-songwriter.

Stanphill continued, "It was introduced in Europe by a youth group from First Baptist Church of Dallas, Texas. It soon spread over Europe. Some years later, as I visited Nepal, I heard a group from England, also visiting in Nepal, sing my song."

In the lyrics Stanphill explains the happiness that comes to a Christian as his behavior is changed and as he begins to live in the favor of the Lord. The theme of the first verse is "to know the Savior." In the "bridge" of the song Stanphill explains that "real joy" can be possible for a Christian, even in the face of sadness or distress. He speaks of the Christian life as a relationship with the Lord as we make the "trip that leads to heaven."

Reflection

If only everyone in the world could know the joy that comes through having a personal relationship with Christ. One of the most sought after things in the life of people is personal joy. Truly, happiness can only come as we know the Savior.

28

Lost! So Near to Safety

'Til the Storm Passes By

Psalm 107:13–34

*Then they cry unto the LORD in their trouble, and
he bringeth them out of their distresses.*

*M*osie Lister says of his song "'Til the Storm Passes By," "A
man in New York whom I had known called one day and asked
me to write a song for Mahalia Jackson." (Mrs. Jackson was especially popular for her rendition of "He's Got the Whole World in
His Hands.") Lister had grown up with people of minority groups,
so when Mahalia Jackson's name was mentioned, he remembered
something of her background. He felt, too, that the right kind of
song for her would fall perfectly into place in his mind. The song
Lister wrote contains the prayers of struggling people.

"I feel that this is something God gave me to say," Lister
explains. "Strangely enough, we could never get [Mahalia Jack-
son] to sing it but, of course, a lot of other people sang it. The
man who so very much wanted me to write it was never able to
do with it what he wanted, but still God used it."

The song has been a blessing to millions, including some
Baptist missionaries who were camping a few years ago on a
tiny island off the coast of New Guinea. They had gone there
for an outing, a day of relaxation. The island was named Mbil
Mbil and was only about three miles in circumference.

During the day, the group exhausted their supply of drinking water, so several volunteered to take the boat to the base island of New Guinea and bring back some water. The trip to the base island was without incident, but the return trip was quite a different story.

They had no sooner filled their containers and boarded the boat when thunder clouds began to roll in. They pushed the throttle to full-speed-ahead and made toward Mbil Mbil, but the storm fell on them like a giant monster. The sky grew black and foreboding. The wind became so strong and the waves so tempestuous, the boat and all its passengers were in jeopardy. Because steering the boat was impossible, they were forced to turn the bow of the boat into the waves and try just to keep the engine running.

The occupants of the boat began to pray fervently that God would spare their lives and guide them toward the tiny island, or at least toward land of some kind. All of a sudden, one of the fellows said, "Why don't we praise Him?" Then, as the waves rolled and the wind howled about them, they sang, "'Til the Storm Passes By."

They later reported that God's presence filled the boat. "We knew He was there. Our hearts were cheered. All of a sudden, one saw a flickering light on the island." Those who had remained on the island had sensed their companions' problem and had gone to the shore with a strong light. Eventually the storm-tossed passengers made it to safety on the island.

Although there was a small prayer meeting on the shore that night, the next morning the whole group met together for worship service. They studied God's Word afresh and anew, and recognized in a more real sense how man is often lost in the storms of life and must always look to the heavenly Father for guidance. Old truths took on new meanings. They already knew what it meant to be lost in the darkness of sin and then saved by the Light of the World, but this reality carried more impact because of their experience the night before.

If you know Jesus Christ as Savior, then you, like those missionaries, must keep in mind that others are still lost on the sea of darkness and sin. They need His light to bring them safely to shore.

Reflection

We cannot fully appreciate the security of knowing Christ until we, through reading the Scriptures, become acutely aware that many are in need of rescue and cannot find their way to Him. We can shine a beacon and guide them to the Lord Jesus Christ.

29

Much More to Come

Mansion over the Hilltop

Luke 12:27–34

*Fear not, little flock; for it is your Father's good
pleasure to give you the kingdom.*

A young businessman stood to give his testimony concerning God's blessings in his life. It was 1945 during a revival meeting in Dallas, Texas. The evangelist was Gene Martin, and in the audience was a famous songwriter, Ira Stanphill.

The young man stated that his business had been on the decline for some time, and it looked as if he would go completely under. This man shared that he was a Christian and knew that the Lord had saved him, yet he did not understand why the Lord would allow these things to happen in his life. He was not accustomed to such financial reverses, and had been thrust more and more into the depths of despair.

Then one day, for diversion or relaxation, he got into his car and drove into the country. He drove for miles out beyond the busy streets and residential areas, where he stopped his car on a lonely road and continued on foot. He happened upon a deserted, out-of-the-way trail and eventually came to a dilapidated cottage. It was in sad disrepair with half the windows broken. Out front was a small girl who played with a broken doll. Although the stuffing in the doll was protruding in several places, the child seemed to be content and happy.

He eased up to the front yard and called the little girl over. "Little girl, how can you be happy living in such a house as that? It is broken down, the windows are out in many places, and that doll that you have in your hand is broken and the stuffing is coming out. How can you be happy?" The little girl looked up with her big, bright eyes and said, "Mister, you see, my daddy just came into a lot of money and he is building us a brand new mansion over that hilltop."

The young businessman testified that those words pierced his heart. He realized for the first time that, although his earthly business was in shambles, the heavenly Father had much greater things in store for him. It was as though he heard God Himself saying, "Son, don't you know that I have a mansion prepared for you just beyond those clouds?" The young man concluded his story, telling how he went back home with a new determination to live for God, let God take care of his business, and to look toward eternal things.

After hearing that young man speak, Ira Stanphill went home and to bed that night, but rose early the next morning and went to his piano. With that story from the night before still fresh in his mind, he wrote the song "Mansion over the Hilltop." It has gone all across the country, into all of our churches and into our homes, and has been recorded by scores of recording artists.

The Bible says that it has not even entered the heart of man, nor can we even conceive, all of the things that God has prepared for those who love Him (see 1 Cor. 2:9). You may live in a humble home or even a small shack or cottage, but God has prepared greater and more beautiful things. We know that He has, because He says so in His Word. So don't be discouraged.

Many of us would be hard pressed to sing Stanphill's song with sincerity, especially the part of the lyric that says that we're satisfied with "just a cottage," or a "little silver," or a "little gold." The stanza that states that we are often "tormented and tested," or have no permanent dwelling here on earth, is more realistic for most of us.

Reflection

Nothing is judged superior except by comparison. Thus, we will not fully realize the excellence of all that God has prepared for us until we are able to compare it with what we now have on the earth.

30

Not in the Mood for God to Use Me

Fill My Cup, Lord

John 4:5–29

The woman saith unto him, Sir, give me this water,
that I thirst not, neither come hither to draw.

The year was 1925, and a young American woman gave birth to a son in Chungking, China. This child's parents were medical missionaries, and the little boy would grow up to bless the hearts of millions of people—for years to come. His name was Richard Blanchard.

When young Richard was less than five years of age, his parents were driven from China in the wake of a mighty Communist onslaught. The young couple and their child were brought to the United States, where they lived in Indiana. As the child grew, he became tremendously interested in music, especially the trombone. The late Homer Rodeheaver, song leader for Billy Sunday and friend of Richard's parents, paid fifty dollars down on a trombone for young Blanchard, who was to finish paying for it with money earned from a paper route.

In ensuing years, Richard served a hitch in the Navy, earned degrees from Mercer and Emory Universities, and then was called to a pastorate in the United Methodist Church. In the years that followed, Blanchard pastored several of the largest Methodist churches in the state of Florida.

Life was never to be a bed of roses for Richard. A severe lung problem developed, and he was faced with two major operations that left him with only one-third of his lung capacity and an unswerving faith in God. But his diminished physical condition did not stop young Blanchard.

In 1953, he embarked on a television ministry, *Horizons of Faith,* seen on a Miami station for seven years. During this time he became the pastor of a church in Coral Gables, Florida.

It was while at that church that Blanchard was asked by a young couple to perform their marriage ceremony. He agreed to do so and had them come to his office for counseling sessions. When the time came for the second session, the couple was quite late for their appointment. Angered that they would be late for the session, Blanchard told his secretary, "I'll wait for thirty minutes and I'm leaving." He then went to a nearby Sunday school classroom and sat down to play the piano. He later said, "When I was not in the mood to be used of God, God was in a mood to use me." In less than thirty minutes, as he waited for the young couple, God gave to him, like a flowing fountain, the beautiful and inspiring "Fill My Cup, Lord."

Blanchard introduced the song to Bill Mann following a revival service in Fort Lauderdale, Florida. They were in a layman's home and Bill Mann sang it while Blanchard accompanied him on the piano. Two years later, in 1964, Mann recorded it on a Word record. It rapidly soared in popularity, and since then, more than one hundred million copies of the song have been sold in sheet music form.

Bill Mann was once singing for a crusade in one of England's largest concert halls when someone approached him before one of the services and said, "The Prime Minister's wife, Mrs. Harold Wilson, would like to make a request. Would you sing a song for her?" Mann quickly agreed to do so, and her request was "Fill My Cup, Lord."

According to his own testimony, Blanchard's lyrics are not at all consistent with his mood at the time. It's difficult to understand how God could drop such meaningful lyrics into a heart filled with anger. Only the Lord knows how the reference to the "woman at the well" came into Blanchard's heart at that moment. One can only conclude that the Lord answered a longing in Blanchard's heart—"fill my cup." His admission to the "thirsting of my soul" is more consistent with his general frame of mind during those moments spent sitting at the piano waiting for the young couple.

As Richard Blanchard looked back over his life, he declared to me, "Even though God chose to impair my physical being, He has in so many ways 'filled my cup.'"

Reflection

Have you been in a mood lately to be used of God? God is constantly ready to use you. Surrender to Him completely today and He will satisfy your longings and direct your pathway.

31

Not Yet, But I'm Fixin' To

Holy Ground

Ephesians 2:14–22

*In whom all the building fitly framed together
groweth unto an holy temple in the Lord: in whom
ye also are builded together for an habitation of
God through the Spirit.*

*O*ccasionally, a songwriter's work is so blessed of the Lord
that his or her songs become meaningful to Christians around
the world. In most cases these individuals started their journey
into the world of Christian music in early childhood.

Geron Davis was born into a pastor's home in Bogalusa,
Louisiana, in 1960. His dad, Gerald, is still pastoring to this
day. Geron related his story to me.

"I was raised around music. My mom, Patricia Davis, played
piano, my dad played the guitar, and they sang together. I often sang with them, even at ages four and five. They would
stand me on a piano bench behind the pulpit, and I would sing
the melody while Mom sang alto and Dad sang tenor and played
his guitar. I started making up songs as a small child, simple
choruses that we would sing in Sunday school. I would often sit
at the piano and try to pick out tunes because I listened to a lot
of music."

In his early teens, Geron seriously started to write songs. To this date he has written more than two hundred songs that are published by companies such as Integrity Music, Gaither Music, Benson, and Word, just to name a few.

Following is Geron Davis's story behind his most famous song:

"When I was nineteen years of age my dad was pastor of a church in Savannah, Tennessee. The church had progressed and grown to the point that a new sanctuary was needed. When we were about two months from the completion of a beautiful new church auditorium, my dad asked, 'Son, would you write a song for us to sing during the first service in our new building?' I replied, 'OK, Dad.' Well, a couple of weeks went by and I had not written the song. My dad asked, 'Son, how about it? Do you have a song for us?' I said, 'No, Dad, but I'll write one.'

"I was busy traveling from place to place, singing with some of the young people from our church. Dad had purchased us a van, a trailer, and a sound system. We sang in churches all around our area. I was also busy writing songs for the group to sing. But Dad was insistent; he desperately wanted me to write the song for the new building. He kept bugging me. I was like, 'Dad, just chill out, I'll write a song.'

"Well Saturday night came, the night before the first service in the new building, and I still had not written a song. We had worked all day at the church getting everything ready. It wasn't a large church, only a couple hundred members, but people were there working, putting last minute touches on everything.

"After all of the church members had gone, and only Dad, Mom, and I were left, we began to check all of the Sunday school rooms and the offices, making sure that those areas of the church complex were in readiness for the big day. My dad turned to me and asked, 'Do you have a song for us?' I used a good ole southern term and said, 'No, Sir, but I'm fixin' to.'

"I went into the new sanctuary, dimmed the lights and sat down at the new grand piano. I began to think, *What do we want to say when we come into this building tomorrow to have a service for the first time?* I began to hum a bit and softly sing some lyrics that were coming to me. As I began to write the lyrics down they kept coming about as fast as I could write. Within fifteen minutes I had finished the entire song. I then went home and to bed. Someone asked me later, 'Did you realize that you had written something powerful?' To which I replied, 'Are you kidding? I was nineteen years old, it was midnight, and I wanted to get to bed.' I was too young to recognize the greatness of what God had done. I was just happy the song was finished.

"I'm the oldest of four kids. I knew that I could be a little bossy with the younger children, so I got two of them up early the next morning and taught them all of the parts to my new song. We sang it later that morning in the church service."

The depths of the lyrics are amazing, considering they came from the heart and mind of a lad so young. I'm sure he was picturing in his thoughts the crowds who would gather with their needs "in His presence" the following morning. Of course, Geron knew that "He has the answer," and that they could reach out and claim the solutions to their problems.

They had all spent so much time and effort in giving, working, and preparing for the new sanctuary where the Word of God would be preached, Davis surely thought of it as a place where the Spirit of the Lord would work in the hearts of those who were in need—a hallowed place, "in His presence."

"My dad was happy because we had a song. My mom cried because she thought her kids never sounded better. The congregation responded unbelievably to the song. I said to myself, *Well, it's a highly emotional day*. It was our first Sunday in the new building, and we appreciated what had happened, but we had no idea what would really happen to the song over the coming years. Even so, the events of the morning made for a memorable birth for my song."

I asked Geron, "How much of the song did you have written down in order to teach your brother and sister their parts?" He replied, "Only the lyrics. I taught each of them their parts by rote. I've always been an arranger at heart, so, as we sat around the piano that morning, I taught them the arrangement of the song that I had retained in my head." Geron's brother, Jeff, was seventeen and his sister Alyson was eleven. A younger sister was only six years old. "My sister Alyson is now married," said Geron, "and she and her husband, Shelton Lovern, travel and sing with us full time."

As Geron and his brother and sister continued to sing "Holy Ground," it so grew in popularity that it was used during the funeral of President Clinton's mother. Barbara Streisand, who was in attendance at the funeral, was so taken by the song, she recorded it and put it on her next CD. It's been recorded by hundreds, if not thousands, of singing groups, and shows no signs of slowing in ascent as it becomes one of the most popular and well-known Christian songs in the world.

Reflection

In whatever situation we find ourselves, it is a place of service to Christ. Letting our lives count for Him, in whatever location, should be our goal. He is with us, and in His presence there is fullness of joy. Live today as if you are truly standing on holy ground.

32

One Song Gave Birth to Another

Wedding Music

Revelation 19:1–9

*Blessed are they which are called unto the marriage
supper of the Lamb.*

Kirk Talley's name is synonymous with Southern Gospel Music. He has made a threefold contribution to that genre of Christian music—as a singer, a songwriter, and a promoter of the works of other songwriters. He was very instrumental, for example, in bringing the songs of Dianne Wilkinson to the attention of Glenn Payne and the Cathedrals.

Talley's experiences are legendary, first as a member of a family singing group; then as first tenor with the Hoppers, the Cathedrals, and the Trio; and as a soloist and writer of songs. But the major portion of his Christian influence will forever be his songwriting—the blending of a biblical message with a beautiful melody. When the voice of Kirk Talley is at last silent, his songs will live on in the hearts of Christians as they continue to worship God using his musical creations.

Although known primarily as a Southern Gospel musician, Talley has crossed into other areas of Christian music, making major contributions with songs such as "Triumphantly the Church Shall Rise" and "Magnify Him," to name only two.

Kirk was born into a musical home in Whitesburg, Tennessee.

"My dad was a song leader and my brother was a pianist," Kirk said. "So we sang. My dad taught me to sing first tenor before I could read. We sang locally at our little church, Shady Grove Free Will Baptist Church in Whitesburg, when we were growing up."

Kirk came to know the Lord at age thirteen at his home church. He said, "After the preacher had given his sermon, he gave an invitation for people to receive Christ. The Lord spoke to my heart. I knew I needed to walk the aisle and trust Christ as my Savior, and that is what I did. And you know, it was the best thing that ever happened to me."

His songwriting abilities were manifested early. He wrote his first song, "When I See His Face," at age fifteen. Several groups recorded the song, including the Hoppers, the Dixie Melody Boys, and the Cathedral Quartet. He reports that he has written somewhere in the neighborhood of two hundred songs.

The writing of "Wedding Music" was the result of a surprising series of events.

"'Wedding Music' was actually a spin-off of 'Triumphantly the Church Shall Rise,' another song I had written years before," said Kirk. "Our family sang that song one night at a church in Louisiana. It caused a good reaction among the people. They were excited. After we had finished singing, the preacher got up and said, 'You know, the church will rise and we will see Jesus. We will take part in a wedding, the marriage supper of the Lamb.' Then he added, 'I believe I hear wedding music!' That phrase jumped out at me, and I knew I had the theme for another song.

"A couple of weeks later I was visiting in the home of Phil Cross—another songwriter—in Chattanooga, Tennessee. We went to his music room and I shared my thoughts with him about the prospects of a new song. We began working on the idea, first at the piano and then sitting in opposite corners of the room, bouncing ideas off of each other. We would write a line or two and then give those ideas further thought. We continued that way until we had finished 'Wedding Music.'

"Sometime later I was on a cruise to Alaska. Gerald Wolfe, at that time with the Cathedrals, was also there, and we were sitting around the piano singing. I sang 'Wedding Music,' and he replied, 'Man that's a good song! The Cathedrals ought to cut that one.' I put it on a tape for him to present to Glenn Payne and the others of the group. They recorded it, and it went to number one on the charts and remained there for three months."

Kirk continues to travel on the Southern Gospel circuit and is a favorite everywhere he ministers in song.

Reflection

I daresay that when we think of sitting around the table at the marriage supper of the Lamb, we don't usually think of singing. But what would a wedding in heaven be like without singing a song of praise in the presence of and to our wonderful Savior and Lord?

33

Remembering Childhood Prayers

How Long Has It Been?

Ephesians 6:10–24

*Praying always with all prayer and supplication in
the Spirit, and watching thereunto with all perse-
verance and supplication for all saints.*

"'How Long Has It Been?' is the greatest gospel song." That
was the declaration of Albert E. Brumley. Someone asked him,
"What about 'I'll Fly Away,' your song?" Mr. Brumley answered,
"It's not in the same class."

Mosie Lister once said, "I sweat blood over most of the songs
I write. I work hard at making them what I think they ought to
be. But 'How Long Has It Been?' was one of those rare excep-
tions that almost seemed to write itself. It came to me quickly
and easily. The writing took a little more than ten minutes."

I first met Mosie Lister in 1958 in Tampa, Florida, where I
visited with him in his home. He told me the story of how he
wrote his most famous song. From that interview—and from
material published by Lillenas Publishing Company who
publishes Mosie's choral arrangements, musicals, and song
collections—comes the following story:

"I grew up in a Christian home and was taught to say my
prayers before going to bed—'Now I lay me down to sleep' and
other childhood petitions. We also learned to express to God

in other ways. It occurred to me one day that there were no doubt many adults who grew up with that kind of experience as children. I wondered if I couldn't say something in a song that would ask if they still remembered that God heard those prayers; if they remembered telling God, 'I love you.' I thought about asking, 'How long has it been since you prayed like that? How long since you really prayed?'

"All of a sudden I realized that this was what I needed to say. I just started writing as fast as I could. I had the words and the music in a little more than ten minutes, and before much longer had the whole song completed. Later I felt disappointed with one chord and changed it, but that was the only change I made."

He placed the song on the top of the upright piano and went about chores for the day, not thinking a great deal more about it. Yet, in five years, it had sold more than one million copies in sheet music form and was recorded by numerous recording artists.

George Beverly Shea, America's beloved gospel singer and famed soloist associated with Billy Graham, told me after one of the Graham services in Tampa, Florida, that for a number of years he closed his concerts with Mosie's song, "How Long Has It Been?"

Since 1955, and after several different jobs in the music field and a hitch in the Navy, Mosie has devoted his life to the writing of gospel songs and hymns. In 1969 Mosie Lister Publications merged with Lillenas Publishing Company; administrative and distribution duties gave way to full concentration on creativity. (More about Lister's life is given in other stories in this volume.)

Mosie said, "I think God has directed my thoughts on certain occasions toward writing songs. I don't think my songs would have gone as well as they have if God hadn't directed. I prayed that God would use what talent I had to bring some blessing to other people."

In 1976, Mosie Lister was inducted into the Gospel Music

Hall of Fame. His songs are an accurate and genuine reflection of a vital and growing relationship with God Himself. A desire to equip the saints and a passion to honor God—that's the heart of Mosie Lister.

In the lyrics of this song Mosie asks not only, "How long has it been since you talked with the Lord?" but he teaches Christians that Christ will hear you when you pray and will keep you through the long nights of loneliness and trouble. These things cause the mind to feel at ease and make the day worth living. Thanks, Mosie, for those questions and those instructions in Christian living.

Reflection

What was your answer to the question in this song? How long has it been since you were burdened about a friend or loved one and prayed until God heard and answered? How long since you rose from your knees a victorious Christian? Make today your day to renew your vow to pray as you ought. Take advantage of this wonderful power in your life!

34

The Little Lake Song

A Perfect Heart

Psalm 119:9–16

With my whole heart have I sought thee: O let me
not wander from thy commandments. Thy word
have I hid in mine heart, that I might not sin
against thee.

*W*hat a thrill for Dony and Reba Rambo McGuire! They
arrived at a large gathering in Zimbabwe, Africa, where thousands of happy Christians sang one of their beautiful songs,
first in their native language and then in charming, heavily
accented English. Reba reports, "I was so moved that I was
reduced to an emotional basket case for a few moments." That
song, "A Perfect Heart," was born several years before on Cen-
ter Hill Lake, near Nashville, Tennessee.

Reba, an only child born October 17, 1951, in Madisonville,
Kentucky, to Buck and Dottie Rambo, began her musical career very early. She relates, "From my earliest recollection there
were guitars, pianos, mandolins, and banjos around. Music has
been a constant with me during my whole life. I began traveling with my parents at thirteen years of age and have been
traveling ever since." She and her husband, Dony, now bring
their ministry to thousands in many churches and auditoriums.

Dony was born in Tulsa, Oklahoma, in 1951, one of seven

children. He studied music for many years—in high school, college, and beyond. Beginning his songwriting in 1975, he has written both on his own and in association with such notables as Gloria Gaither and his wife, Reba. Dony was an accomplished pianist, songwriter, and recording artist before his marriage to Reba in 1980.

The story behind "A Perfect Heart" begins when friends invited the McGuires to vacation with them on their houseboat on a lake near Nashville. They had determined to work diligently on their songwriting during that time, and they did so. They prayed earnestly that the Lord would do something special through them that week. At the end of the week they had completed a number of songs and done some work on a musical. Reba tells the story.

"On the very last morning we were to be on the boat, Dony got up very early to try to catch a catfish for breakfast. He's an early riser. I was so full of faith in his fishing ability that I proceeded to the kitchen and started to cook bacon and eggs.

"The sun was peeking over the hills and a mist was rising from the water. It was a glorious morning. I looked out of a small porthole and caught a glimpse of Dony with a strange look on his face. Some people come down with a cold, while Dony comes down with a song! I couldn't explain it, but I knew something good was about to happen. I turned off the burners where I was cooking and removed the food. I gathered our songwriting materials and sat down to wait for him to come in.

"When he came in a few minutes later, he sat down before a small electric piano and began to play. As he played what the Lord was giving to him, I began to write lyrics as they were being given to me. That kind of inspiration had only occurred a few times in our short songwriting career together. It was as if God was saying, 'You've been faithful in your praying and studying for a week, now I'm going to give you something just because I have the power to do so.' I wrote as fast as I could write while Dony continued to play. We both completed the whole composition and have never changed a word or the musical setting.

"It became our 'little lake song.' We used it for a time around our offices as a devotional song and sang it at a few small churches. One day Bill Gaither came by our offices and heard us singing it during one of our devotional periods. He asked where we got it. We told him it was our 'lake song.' He expressed such a keen interest in it that Dony made a tape of it for him. That started it on its way."

And so, several years later, halfway around the world in Zimbabwe, the McGuires heard their "little lake song" being sung by the great host of Africans gathered there.

Reflection

The Lord will always reward your faithful attention to His leading. It may not be with a song, but it will be with His choice of some good work you can do for Him.

35

The Old Is Still New

Cornerstone

Ephesians 2:11–22

*Now therefore ye are no more strangers and foreign-
ers, but fellowcitizens with the saints, and of the
household of God; and are built upon the foundation of the apostles and prophets, Jesus Christ
himself being the chief corner stone.*

*M*illions of people have been blessed by the music of Lari
Goss, although many didn't know who Lari Goss was. He has
orchestrated and conducted the accompaniment for more Christian recordings than almost any other person living today. But
it was not until Lari had reached a pinnacle of music acclaim
among Christian musicians that the Lord decided to use him
to send a melody around the world.

Lari was born to wonderful Christian parents in Cartersville,
Georgia, in 1945. Although he started singing with his family
as a child, he was not given the opportunity of extensive music
training. Lari is self-taught, but what a musician! His abilities
are in demand by the leading music publishers of our day.

As a teenager Lari and his brothers, James and Roni, sang as
a trio. Their harmonies were so close and unusual they were
considered by leading musicians of the day to be far ahead of
their time. At Southern Gospel concerts they usually started

the performances or were the last to sing. Other singing groups had a greater appreciation of their abilities than did the audiences, who were not as musical. Backstage it was a common sight to see groups of singers gathered around them to hear their awesome harmonies and chord progressions.

Lari began orchestrating songs at the age of sixteen, conducting his first recording session with thirty-five symphony players.

I had the privilege of working closely with Lari for a period of time in Marietta, Georgia, where I was Minister of Music and Lari was the pianist. I soon realized that I had never met a musician with more creativity and talent.

Lari related the following story to me:

"I had a melody that the Lord had given me that I called 'Cornerstone.' Yet, I had no lyrics. At the same time I was studying the Word. [Lari is a conscientious student of the Bible.] I had been reading in the Scriptures where Jesus is presented as the chief Cornerstone. I reasoned with myself that maybe I could put that thought with my melody. The lyrics of the song came strictly from the inspiration of the Word of God. Most all of the phrases in the song are straight Scripture.

"I continued to work the melody and the Scriptures into each other. Then I went to the old hymnals to see what former writers had to say about Christ as a Stone or the Rock of our salvation. I borrowed a line from an old hymn—I don't even remember the song—'Where the seeds of truth are sown.' Then I turned to that old favorite song, 'Rock of Ages.' It so ably depicts Christ as the Cornerstone, the Rock of Ages. My mind then went to our security in the Lord. That led me to 'Rock of Ages, so secure, for all time it shall endure. 'Til His children reach their home, He remains the Cornerstone.'

"No event or incident in my life influenced the song. It is strictly from the Scriptures."

Nancy Harmon, the noted traveling singer, was the first to record it about two years after Goss had written it. It was nominated for a Dove Award in 1978 and still continues to be a favorite everywhere.

Reflection

No matter what your lot in life, if you are a Christian you are secure in the knowledge that the Lord Jesus Christ is the foundation and support of your very existence.

36

They Didn't Believe Him, Either

Follow Me

1 Peter 5:1–11

Casting all your care upon him;
for he careth for you.

The young newlywed lay very ill and discouraged. The tiny shack in which she lay stood on the back side of a mission compound in Africa. She and her husband, a young medical doctor, had left the United States to go to that part of the world as missionaries.

They had struggled for months, building living quarters, pulling teeth, doctoring ulcers, caring for the African nationals. Day after day they came with their problems and cares.

The young doctor ministered to their medical needs as he witnessed to them, trying to win them to Christ. He soon saw that, while he was able to help them physically, he was not seeing souls come to know Christ. That was, after all, their major reason for coming to this place.

To add to the missionary's anxiety, his wife was sick and lay all day long in their little shack. The hardship and the struggle became too great, and he began to give in to the pressures. His cry to God became, "Lord, get me out of this and I'll go back to the United States and be faithful to You. I'll pastor a small church and do Your work. I just want to leave this place. I want my wife to be well. I still want to serve You, but not here. I'm a failure in this mission field. I'm not seeing people saved. I seem to be spending all my time pulling teeth and caring for the medical needs, so let me go back home, please."

Suddenly the picture changed, the missionary explained. "It seemed that I could almost see Christ with the wounds in His hands. His message was so plain. His words to me were, 'I preached, in the streets of Jerusalem, the same message that you are giving to these people, and they didn't believe me, either. Why don't you just follow me and leave the results in my hands?'"

The once-despairing young physician did just that. He received tremendous spiritual strength from the Lord's message to him. He soon began to see people saved, and his wife became well again. And out of the darkness came little sunbeams shining all around them. They became two of the greatest missionaries that their particular board had ever sent to the continent of Africa.

That story was given one night by Dr. Charles Greenaway in a missionary conference in Grand Prairie, Texas. He and his wife, Mary, were the missionaries that had gone to Africa many years before.

Ira Stanphill, the talented songwriter, was sitting in the audience. He was so moved by the story he went home weeping. The next morning he went to his piano and, with tears streaming down his face, penned the song, "Follow Me."

In the song he likens the Christian life to one of loneliness, with people engaged in the work of the Lord often unnoticed and unappreciated. Then in the song, Christ reminds us that He, too, underwent hardships while on this earth. He understands and gives the tender instruction, "Just lift your cross and stay real close to Me."

The final verse has caused the song to be a favorite among missionaries. It begins with the prospect of one dying on a "foreign field some day." It goes on to reveal that no matter what a Christian on a mission field endures, it is all done in the love of Christ. The song closes with the determined proclamation of a Christian who takes his cross and follows close to Jesus.

God does not always provide an easy life for us, but His message to us is the same as to the apostle Paul: "My grace is sufficient for thee" (2 Cor. 12:9). Although we, like Paul, may implore the Lord to deliver us from trials and tribulations, He may be using these things to harden us, make us strong and useful servants in His loving hands. We need only to heed that awesome challenge: "Follow Me."

Reflection

Never forget that God sees you, knows all about you, and cares for you. Your extremity is His opportunity to forge you into the person He wants you to be.

37

Thirteen Cents on the Contract

Remind Me, Dear Lord

Psalm 143

*I remember the days of old; I meditate on all thy
works; I muse on the work of thy hands.*

*E*arly in the music ministry of Dottie Rambo, God unmistakably showed her direction. When the way ahead was foggy, God chose what would be to some an insignificant act to guide her decision making. Consider Dottie's story about her song "Remind Me, Dear Lord," as she told it to me.

"At the time I wrote this song, we were living in Kentucky just getting started in the music ministry. I was holding down a job and singing on the weekends. I received a call from John T. Benson. We called him 'Pop.' He called about having me sign a writer's contract and about having our family sing for him. We didn't know about contracts or what to do about such things. Since it was only a hundred miles from Nashville, my family and I drove to see Pop Benson.

"As we traveled I prayed: 'Lord, we don't know anything about contracts, so You will have to lead us. If we are to sign the contract, let it read so many hundred dollars and thirteen cents. If You'll just let thirteen cents be the last numbers on the contract, then I'll know that we are supposed to sign it.' I told no one about my prayer.

"When we arrived we began to look over the contract. I was tying to find out the amount. I said, 'Let me look at it.' Mr. Benson looked over his glasses and said, 'Well, Dot, my girl, this is the best I can do.' I really wasn't interested in anything except that *thirteen cents.* When I looked at the amount, it read so many dollars and *thirteen cents!* When I saw that I said, 'Give me a pencil.' There was a mild protest, 'Wait a minute, we haven't read it that well. We don't know that much about it.' I said, 'We don't need to know anything else. We're just supposed to sign it.' So we signed it.

"We got into our car and began pulling away from the curb. All of a sudden, I began talking quietly to the Lord. I said, 'Lord, I appreciate You doing this for me. I know You must have done a million things like this that I didn't know about or don't remember, and haven't thanked You for, but You know me—I'm human and I forget. But when You do good things, just roll back the curtain and remind me of them and I'll thank You for them!'

"When that happened the melody in my heart started rolling and I started weeping. I was asked, 'What's wrong with you?' I said, 'Nothing, I'm just rejoicing. I'm writing a song.' During the one hundred miles home, without an instrument, I wrote 'Remind Me, Dear Lord.'"

In the song, Dottie reveals the unusual talent she has received from the Lord—a unique insight into human character, played out in the life of a Christian. She teaches each of us to occasionally let the Lord "roll back the curtain" of our memory and remind us that all we have accomplished is because of God's goodness. She also reminds us of our humanness and our frailty.

Reflection

A deplorable weakness in us is our forgetfulness of His blessings and His watchful care. May we do all in our power to break this habit by often opening our hearts to His loving reminders.

38

Three Chords and a Cloud of Dust

Boundless Love

John 3:16–21

*For God so loved the world, that he gave his only
begotten Son, that whosoever believeth in him
should not perish, but have everlasting life.*

*D*ianne Wilkinson loves her Southern heritage, her Southern Baptist church, and her Southern Gospel Music. But not necessarily in that order. She was born in Blytheville, Arkansas, in 1944, a hop, skip, and a jump from Memphis, Tennessee. Memphis is the home of Ellis Auditorium, where she was exposed to Southern Gospel Music while still a very young child. She was often carried there by her mother and her mother's sister.

Her grandmother—with whom she, her mother, and her brother lived—had an upright piano in her home. One day she announced to Dianne, at that time about eight years of age, "OK, you are going to start piano lessons." She did so, and her progress on the piano was so rapid that by the time she was twelve she was playing for church services. Her piano playing and her singing improved to the point that she joined her mother and her aunt as a trio. The Ross Sisters, as they called themselves, traveled around singing in churches and on radio programs.

When she was a young adult, a very important event took place in Dianne's life. She related the following to me:

"In 1974, when I was thirty, the Lord began to deal with me that I had never really been saved. I said to the Lord, 'Oh, no Lord, I teach Sunday school, I play the piano for a Baptist church,' and I really loved church. I loved the Lord in the only way that a person in my place in life could. I wrestled with that and was under great conviction for several weeks, feeling that I could talk to no one about it. But I finally threw up a big white flag of surrender and gave my whole heart to the Lord. I was saved and baptized at that time."

Dianne and her husband, Tim, borrowed a thousand dollars to have a quality demo tape produced, presenting a number of her best songs at the time, one of which was "Boundless Love." She said of the song, "It is just one of those good old songs—like George Younce says, 'just three chords and a cloud of dust.'"

Shortly after it was written it was predicted that "Boundless Love" would be the song that would bring her name to the forefront of Southern Gospel Music.

The Wilkinsons took the demo tape to the Southern Quartet Convention and there met Kirk Talley, tenor singer in the Cathedrals Quartet, and gave him a copy of the tape. Talley immediately took great interest in the songs and helped bring about a relationship between Wilkinson and the Cathedrals that would last for almost twenty years. In all, the Cathedrals recorded sixteen of her songs. Dianne added, "Because I worked full-time in the healthcare business, I didn't have a great deal of time to promote my music. I was fortunate enough to have my songs be a part of that Cathedral rising meteor."

Dianne wrote "Boundless Love" in the early 1970s, and the family group with which she sang used it extensively in Blytheville for a number of years. But, because it was on the first demo tape given to Kirk Talley, the Cathedrals had it in their arsenal of songs. Roger Bennett called Dianne in the mid-1980s and told her that they were going to put her song on the

"Traveling Live" album. Her response to Roger was, "Well, finally you're going to get that good old barn burner on." As it turned out, in 1987, "Boundless Love" was the first number one song that Dianne ever had on the radio charts. In the years that followed, the Cathedrals never dropped it from their program. They also continue to use "We Shall See Jesus." Touring groups and church choirs have caused those two selections to become her most widely used songs, especially since Tom Fettke put them into his choral collections published by Lillenas.

The whole message of the song is tied up in one phrase—"Jesus wants to love you; there is none above you." We will only know when we get to heaven how "precious in His sight" we really are.

Reflection

Love . . . there is no greater or more meaningful word in the English language. Yet it's a word that we understand only in human terms. There is, however, a love that is far beyond our ability to comprehend—the love of God for us. That is "boundless love." It has no beginning or end. You and I were loved by our heavenly Father before "the foundation of the world," and He will love us throughout all eternity.

39

Two Teens, Singing in Calcutta

Thank You (for Giving to the Lord)

2 Corinthians 9:6–15

*Every man according as he purposeth in his heart,
so let him give; not grudgingly, or of necessity: for
God loveth a cheerful giver.*

*O*ccasionally a song comes on the scene that goes right to the core of Christianity. It plays on our heart strings and spurs us to action—to give of ourselves and our money to the ministry of Christ. Such is the subject of this story.

Ray Boltz, a singer and songwriter, has made great strides toward becoming a widely used servant of God. It all started at the Ball Memorial Hospital in Muncie, Indiana, in 1953, where Ray was born to William and Ruth Boltz. During his teen years, in addition to songwriting, he became interested in studying piano, organ, and various woodwind instruments.

Ray joined the Kingsley United Methodist Church at age twelve, but his heart was not changed. In his late teen years he became enamored with rock music and what he perceived as unfairness in our society. The Woodstock culture and the protesting of the Vietnam War were foremost in his mind. He stated in an interview, "At age nineteen, I was kind of messed up on drugs and alcohol. I had really gone in the wrong direction. Then one day I attended a Christian concert by a group called

Fishermen from Anderson University. At that concert I made a commitment to the Lord that totally changed my life.

"I had a lot of questions as a teenager about what I saw as injustices and about political issues. But, after I gave my heart to the Lord, I began writing very positive songs about my faith and what Christ had done for me. I finally knew the answer to some of the questions I had been asking.

"In 1987, my wife, Carol, our children, and I were attending the Agape Ministries Church in Muncie. The pastor, Eldon Morehouse, was in a transition period shortly before his retirement. Eldon and I had become very close, and he was a big inspiration to me as I started out in Christian music. He would open the pulpit and allow me to share with the congregation any song that I had written. He encouraged me and empowered me to go out and do what God had called me to do.

"On one occasion as the church was nearing Pastor Appreciation Day, a lady came to me and asked if I would write a song for the special day, which was about eight weeks away. I agreed to do so, but in the following days found myself coming up with absolutely nothing—no ideas at all. I really tried to think of something to say about my pastor—about his visiting the sick, his writing, or his preaching—but nothing seemed to work. This went on for eight weeks. The lady who had asked me to write the song had gone about the church telling people, 'Ray Boltz is writing a very special song for Pastor Appreciation Day.'

"The night before the big day I sat at my piano, praying and seeking the Lord. I said, 'God, you know tomorrow is the day!' At that moment I felt the Lord impressing on my heart that, 'Tomorrow is not appreciation day for your pastor.' I realized that the *real* appreciation day for him and for all Christians is the day we enter into heaven. We can pat people on the back and give them gifts, letting them know we appreciate them, but the real awards for our efforts are going to be handed out in heaven. I knew that Eldon had ministered all during his career to make a difference in eternity.

"So I began to think about heaven and the people in my life who had made a difference. I suddenly realized that very few of those people were famous or were people of power and prestige—people like Sunday school teachers, neighbors, and my mom and dad. I began to write . . . *Thank you for giving to the Lord,* and on and on until I had finished the song, trying to thank people who aren't usually given appreciation.

"The next day I sang it in church. I remember looking over at the pastor as I neared the end of the song and tears were running down his cheeks. I remember thinking, *Well, either I have written a very good song or a very bad song because the pastor is crying.* I soon realized that something had happened, and I knew that if the song blessed his heart then it surely would touch other people. I was sitting at the piano and singing it much as you hear it today, *"Thank you for giving to the Lord. . . ."*

Within twelve months Ray had recorded the song on a new project. "Thank You" was released as a single from that project and went straight to the top of the inspirational and the contemporary charts, becoming one of the top five songs of the year. In 1990 it won a Dove award as Song of the Year.

This song has become a favorite, as might be supposed, among missionaries. Ray stated, "I included the words about the missionaries just to say that many times we don't know what's going to happen with our gifts. I certainly didn't know that this song would be embraced as it has been. I remember when Mother Teresa's funeral was taking place, they brought her body into the big arena there in Calcutta, and as they did so two teenage boys from the Calcutta Assembly of God Church were singing . . . "thank you for giving to the Lord." I had sung in India seven or eight times during mission trips to that country. I met Mother Teresa on one of those trips."

Recognition in addition to the Dove award that has come to Ray Boltz as the writer of this song include nominations for Songwriter of the Year, Album of the Year, and recorded Song of the Year, just to name a few.

Reflection

When you and I stand before the Lord, any task that we have done for Him, any monies that we have given to His work, and any kindness that we have shown to others will receive His recognition and His "well done thou good and faithful servant."

40

Two Tragedies in One Life

When the Saints Go Marching In

Psalm 23

Surely goodness and mercy shall follow me all the days of my life: and I will dwell in the house of the LORD *for ever.*

*J*ames M. Black, born in Scotland in the latter part of the 1800s, became the victim of two tragedies during his lifetime. Yet his days on earth were victorious and fruitful. Between those two terrible events he accomplished many things that live to this present day. Not the least of those accomplishments was his writing the music for a song that has become one of the most famous Christian songs in the United States. The lyrics were written in 1896 by little known poet Katherine Purvis.

At age eight Black was kidnapped. He was later rescued by an elderly minister, who first took the young lad to his home. After finding out more about this terrible event, the minister reunited young Black with his father.

In his early teen years Black became active in various kinds of Christian service. As a young adult he came to America and joined the Epworth League in Williamsport, Pennsylvania, an organization that worked primarily with young people. He later became a Methodist preacher. While still with the Epworth League, Black wrote a gospel song called "When the Roll Is

Called Up Yonder." Although he is well known for that composition, his most famous work is the subject of this story. His unique tune helped launch this perennial favorite.

Louis Armstrong's recording of "When the Saints Go Marching In" on Decca Records in 1948 is credited with the song's popularity and with bringing Armstrong to the forefront of the music world. Many others recorded it, but with much less success.

As the song continues to increase in popularity, we hear it on college campuses, in churches of all sizes, on TV programs of varying kinds, and in gatherings of people of many ethnic origins, young and old. People still gather in Preservation Hall in New Orleans, Louisiana, to listen to the brass bands, who report that this song is their most requested.

One of the managers of Preservation Hall reported to me that the bands became so tired of playing "Saints" that they began charging two dollars to anyone requesting that tune. That move failed to slow the requests down at all. They then increased the fee to five dollars, and the requests kept coming without a let-up. Now ten dollars is charged for requesting the band to play "When the Saints Go Marching In."

A director of a New Orleans funeral home reported that to this day, marching, brass bands can be seen as part of many funeral processions. According to Armstrong in a past interview with a popular magazine, following the burial the brass bands would march back from the cemetery playing some of the popular songs of that day, one of which was, of course, "When the Saints Go Marching In."

It seems that almost every person in the United States can sing at least a portion of the song or hum the tune of the chorus.

> I am just a weary pilgrim,
> trav'ling through this world of sin.
> Getting ready for that meeting,
> when the saints go marching in.

Chorus:
O when the saints go marching in,
when the saints go marching in.
O Lord, I want to be in that number,
when the saints go marching in.

The ministerial activities of Rev. James M. Black were cut short following his untimely death in an automobile accident in Colorado in 1948. This, of course, was the second tragedy in the life of Rev. Black, whose work lives on in the tune he gave us more than a century ago.

Reflection

One phrase of the lyric, "O Lord, I want to be in that number," seems to be sung rather lightly. What does it mean? It means, "Lord, I want to be one of those who will gain entrance into heaven when Christians are entering their eternal home." I'm sure you, too, want to be "in that number"!

A Special Section of Classic Hymns and Gospel Songs Often Recorded and Sung by Southern Gospel Groups

41

A Great Source of Inspiration

In the Garden

John 20:1–18

Jesus saith unto her, Mary. She turned herself, and saith unto him, Rabboni; which is to say, Master.

"*He* looked a little like a southern colonel with his white mustache. And he always appeared at the office with a small flower in his lapel. He had a marvelous sense of humor and a dry wit, which could be very caustic if he thought the occasion demanded it—a truly brilliant man." This is a description of the late C. Austin Miles, given to me by Mrs. H. A. Dye, a friend of Mr. Miles.

His hymn "In the Garden" has become, according to various polls, an extremely popular song in the United States and abroad. More than a million recordings and copies in print form have been sold. It is virtually impossible to pick up a hymnal of any kind and find it omitted. "In the Garden" crosses a lot of lines. It is a favorite, however, of millions of Southern Gospel Music lovers.

Miles's hobby was photography, and he had built his own darkroom. He discovered one day that he could read his Bible in the special light of the darkroom, and he often read passages as he waited for film to be developed. Since he was a songwriter he often read the Bible with the express purpose of getting ideas for gospel songs.

One day in March 1912, Mr. Miles was developing film, and while waiting for this process to complete he picked up his Bible. It fell open to John 20, which records the story of Mary's coming to the garden to visit the tomb of Jesus. As she looked in, her heart sank because He wasn't there. Then as He spoke to her, she recognized Him, and her heart jumped for joy. She cried, "Rabboni!"

Mr. Miles imagined that he was present with them in the garden on that glorious occasion, witnessing the wonderful event. When his thoughts returned to the business at hand in the darkroom, he was gripping his Bible. His muscles, according to his own testimony afterward, were tense and vibrating.

He suddenly realized that we as Christians can experience the presence of Christ in our daily lives. It is constant companionship with Christ that should, in fact, make up the walk of a Christian. In the inspiration of those moments he wrote a poem. He later related that the words came quickly, just as we sing it today. Later that evening he wrote the musical setting.

Mr. Miles often remarked in his later years that he would make it through another year if he could get through the month of March. He didn't like the winds that March often brings, and it is ironic that on March 10, 1946, he passed away in Pitman, New Jersey.

In the lyrics of this great old gospel song Miles expresses the blessedness of close fellowship with the Savior—He walks with me, He talks with me, and He assures me that I belong to Him. What a "joy we share" as we linger in the presence of Christ.

Reflection

Our joy is made perfect as we share that joy with others—the joy of knowing in a personal way the Savior spoken of in the Scripture above. When we seek our own happiness we lose real and satisfying happiness. But when we turn aside to notice the plight of others, and to help, the joy of the Savior will overtake us.

147

42

Assurance

It Is Well with My Soul

Isaiah 48:10–22

*O that thou hadst hearkened to my commandments!
then had thy peace been as a river, and thy righteousness as the waves of the sea.*

Horatio G. Spafford was a successful businessman in Chicago with a lovely family—a wife and five children. The Spaffords were not strangers to sorrow and tragedy. They had lost an infant son to death and much of their business in the great Chicago fire. Yet they had learned that God was in control of every aspect of their lives. The Lord blessed them by allowing the business to flourish again and by giving them other children.

On November 21, 1873, the French ocean liner *Ville du Havre* was crossing the Atlantic from the United States to Europe. On board were Mrs. Spafford and four of the children looking forward to a wonderful holiday. Mr. Spafford had stayed to care for some unexpected business problem but intended to follow the family in a few days on another ship.

About four days into the crossing of the Atlantic, the *Ville du Havre* collided with a powerful iron-hulled English ship, the *Loch Fine*. Suddenly Mrs. Spafford, her four children, and the 221 other passengers were in grave danger. As the panic started, Mrs. Spafford hurriedly brought the four children to the deck.

She knelt there with them and prayed that God would spare them if that could be His will, or to make them willing to endure whatever awaited them. One report says that she thanked the Lord that the children had become Christians just two weeks before.

Within a matter of minutes the ship slipped beneath the dark waters of the Atlantic, carrying with it most of the passengers, including the four Spafford children. A sailor was rowing over the spot where the ship had sunk when he spotted a woman floating on a piece of the wreckage. It was Mrs. Spafford. He pulled her into the boat, and they were picked up by another ship, which landed them in Cardiff, Wales, nine days later. From there she wired her husband this message, "SAVED, ALONE." Mr. Spafford later framed the telegram and hung it in his office.

Spafford booked passage on the next available ship and left to join his heartbroken wife. With the ship about four days out, the captain came to him and told him that, as far as could be determined, the ship was near the spot where his children went down. It is reported that Spafford went to his cabin to rest but could not. He, in his assurance that God is always good, wrote,

> When peace like a river attendeth my way,
> When sorrows like sea billows roll,
> Whatever my lot, Thou hast taught me to say,
> It is well, it is well with my soul.
>
> Chorus:
> It is well with my soul,
> It is well, it is well with my soul.
>
> And Lord haste the day when the faith shall be sight.
> The clouds be rolled back as a scroll,
> The trump shall resound and the Lord shall descend:
> Even so, it is well with my soul.

Spafford later carried his poem to a brilliant young songwriter, Philip P. Bliss, who wrote a moving musical setting that has carried the song around the world. Bliss met tragedy himself when at age thirty-eight he died in a train wreck.

In 1881 Spafford and his wife moved to Jerusalem where they helped build an American colony. They lived there for the remainder of their lives.

Reflection

God will give us His peace when we meet His requirements. Many times He sends unusual circumstances into our lives to make us more like His Son. If all things are accepted as from Him, then His peace is the result.

43

From Heartache to Assurance

No One Ever Cared for Me like Jesus

1 Peter 5:1-7
Casting all your care upon him;
for he careth for you.

"*Let 'er rip!*" was an expression of one of America's foremost gospel songwriters, Dr. Charles F. Weigle. This little expression, odd as it may seem, simply suggests that we not worry about situations over which we have little or no control. Leave it in the hands of God. This godly attitude allowed Weigle to be a blessing and an inspiration to countless thousands of people during his fruitful life. He has written a booklet called *Quit Worrying* that has helped many people with the problems of anxiety.

I had the privilege of knowing Dr. Weigle personally, and even had the opportunity to direct the music in one of his revival campaigns. I was a young song leader and he was an elderly evangelist in his eighties. He lived on the campus of Tennessee Temple University during the latter years of his life. As a student I got to fellowship with him on campus, often sharing meals with him in the dining commons.

Charles Frederick Weigle was born in Lafayette, Indiana, on November 20, 1871. He was converted at the age of twelve. With the help of Christian friends and an unswerving faith in

God, he became a true and faithful laborer for Jesus Christ. Later, he felt the call of God and surrendered to preach the gospel. His life of service to God was enhanced greatly by his ability to write gospel songs.

Dr. Weigle was not without his hours of trouble and heartache. Yet it seems that out of these grievous sorrows flowed forth one of the most beautiful and widely-known of his songs, "No One Ever Cared for Me like Jesus." Phil Kerr, a religious broadcaster on the west coast, reported that requests for it outnumbered requests for any other special gospel song. It has been sung around the world and has been translated into many languages.

One day Dr. Weigle came home to find a note from his wife declaring that she was leaving. She was going to the "world," to get the things that she felt were owed to her. She didn't want to be the wife of an evangelist any longer. This situation threw him into such a state of depression that he actually thought of ending his life. He wondered if anyone cared. At that moment he heard a small voice within saying, "Charlie, I haven't forgotten you. I still care for you." He fell to his knees, asking God to forgive him for not trusting Him completely. He determined never again to let such a thought cross his mind.

In less than five years his wife was dead. While reflecting on the past experiences and the goodness of God, who carried him through the heartache, Weigle felt the urge to once again write a song. The song would be a summation of his whole life experience with his wonderful Lord. He later said that the lyric came as fast as he could put it down. It was the first song he had written since his world fell apart. Now he wanted everyone to know that "No One Ever Cared for Me like Jesus."

Dr. Weigle, in his inspiring lyrics, expresses that he would love to "tell you what I think of Jesus," a Friend that he has found to be strong and true and who has changed his life completely, as no other friend could ever do.

The second is a verse of personal Christian testimony. As

Christians, even if our lives formerly consisted of sin, misery, and woe, Jesus places His arms around us and leads us in the direction that we should go.

The third is the verse of assurance, as we "more and more" understand His love and care—all the way to heaven.

Many stories could be written about the songs of Charles Weigle. In all, he has written four hundred to five hundred, many of which have become very popular among Christians everywhere.

Although this would not ordinarily be considered a "Southern Gospel" song, Edith Tripp has helped make it a favorite among people who particularly love that genre of Christian music.

Reflection

How often have you wondered, "Does anyone really care?" There is One who loves you and cares more for you than you care for yourself. Turn every problem over to Him . . . right now!

44

From the Kitchen Table to the World

The Old Rugged Cross

John 19:13–22

*And he bearing his cross went forth into a place
called the place of a skull, which is called in the
Hebrew Golgotha: where they crucified him,
and two other with him, on either side one,
and Jesus in the midst.*

When polls are taken to determine what are the most popular American hymns, invariably near the top of the list is "The Old Rugged Cross." The popularity of this hymn started during the Billy Sunday campaigns in the earlier parts of this century. Some claim that the song was written between December 29, 1912, and January 12, 1913. It's certain, however, that it is by far the most popular of the approximately three hundred songs written by George Bennard, who lived from 1873 to 1958.

Bennard was born into a very modest family in Youngstown, Ohio. His father passed away during George's teen years, leaving the youth with the responsibility of helping his mother and his brothers and sisters. To that end he became a coal miner like his father before him.

The Salvation Army, which has been a helper of "others" for so many years, was an attraction to Bennard and his young wife, who joined their ranks and worked with the "Army" for a number of years.

Bennard later felt impressed of the Lord to become an itinerant evangelist in a time when it was tough to be on the road. He served for years in Canada and some of our northern states.

Bennard's favorite Scripture verse was John 3:16, which he quoted often. He said that it did not become worn or threadbare to him, with the often quoting of it, but it became more alive and deeper in meaning. He seemed to always have a vision of a cross when quoting the verse—a crude Roman cross stained with the blood of Christ, God's only Son, who gave His life for our salvation.

One day, as he was thinking of that scene, an original melody ran through his mind—"a complete melody," he later reported, but very few words came with it. He struggled to write lyrics, but all that came were the words, "I'll cherish the old rugged cross."

The song seemed to take shape in bits and pieces. He completed the chorus, but the verses did not seem proper and fitting to him. Shortly thereafter he preached in the Friends Church in Sawyer, Wisconsin, and the Methodist Church in Pokagan, Michigan, in the southwest part of the state. During those meetings he sang his song for the people and they responded favorably, but he was not satisfied.

Following the meetings in Pokagan, he was scheduled to speak in New York State and there he majored on the theme of the cross. Numbers of people were trusting in what Christ had done for them on the cross as payment for their sins, confessing Him as their Savior and Lord. Bennard felt that the Lord was revealing to him, in a more meaningful manner, Christ's love as demonstrated at Calvary.

He returned to his home, 1101 E. Michigan Avenue, in Albion, Michigan, thrilled with the experiences in New York and with a renewed meaning of the cross etched into his mind and heart. He went to the kitchen table, took the manuscript that he had so labored over, and in just a short period of time was able to rewrite the stanzas with each word falling perfectly into place. He called his wife and joyfully sang it to her. She loved the song very much.

He then sent the manuscript to Charles H. Gabriel in Chicago, asking him if he would write the proper chords with the melody line. Gabriel did so and returned the song with the message, "You will hear from this song." Others who heard the completed song were also very pleased and made similar predictions.

Bennard said what countless other songwriters say: "I really hadn't written it. I was merely the instrument that God used."

A State of Michigan Historic Site marker stands at the sight on Michigan Avenue in Albion where Bennard wrote the song. It reads,

**BIRTHPLACE OF
"OLD RUGGED CROSS"**
"The Old Rugged Cross," one
of the world's best-loved
hymns, was composed here
in 1912, by the Rev. George
Bennard (1873–1958). The
son of an Ohio coal miner,
Bennard was a lifelong
servant of God, chiefly
in the Methodist ministry.
He wrote the words and
music to over 300 other
hymns. None achieved the
fame of "The Old Rugged
Cross," the moving sum-
mation of his faith.
*"I'll cherish the old rugged cross,
Till my trophies at last I lay down.
I will cling to the old rugged cross,
And exchange it some day for a crown."*

George Bennard lived his retirement years in Reed City, Michigan. It is reported that he felt puzzled that others of his hymns did not become as accepted and used by masses of people as did "The Old Rugged Cross." His last trip to Albion, where he wrote the song, occurred in June 1958, just a few months before his death in October in Reed City. Here is the first verse of his song:

> On a hill far away stood an old rugged cross,
> The emblem of suff'ring and shame.
> And I love that old cross where the dearest and best
> For a world of lost sinners was slain.

Reflection

How marvelous that Christ's cross of shame became to you and me a badge of honor, and the pain and suffering that He endured there was for our eternal deliverance.

45

God's Power Display

How Great Thou Art

Psalm 8

*O Lord our Lord, how excellent is thy name in all
the earth! who hast set thy glory above the heavens.*

"How Great Thou Art" is a song that seems to cross all lines
of Christian musical interpretations and categories. Scores of
Southern Gospel singing groups and soloists have recorded it
and performed it, much to the blessing and delight of those
who hear them.

It was known in several countries before it finally reached
the shores of the United States. The life of this great hymn
began in 1886 on an estate in southern Sweden. A member of
the Swedish parliament and a successful editor walked across
the beautiful grounds of the coastal estate and during his walk
was caught in a thunderstorm. He was in awe as he watched
the sky go from gray to black and then to a beautiful blue
again.

His response to this display of nature was one of adoration
and praise. He later put his thoughts in the form of a poem
that he titled, *"O Store Gud"* (O Great God). It was later set to a
Swedish folk tune. In 1907 Manfred von Glehn translated it
into German, and five years later a Russian pastor, Rev. Ivan
Prokhanoff, translated it into Russian.

Many years later, an English missionary first heard the song in Russia. Stuart Hine, born in 1899, in Hammersmith Grove, a small hamlet in England, was dedicated to the Lord by his parents in a Salvation Army meeting. He was led to Christ by Madame Annie Ryall on February 22, 1914, was baptized shortly thereafter, and was influenced greatly by the teachings of Charles H. Spurgeon.

In 1931, Hine and his young wife went as missionaries to the Carpathian area of Russia, then a part of Czechoslovakia. There, they heard a meaningful hymn, the Russian translation of Carl Boberg's Swedish song.

As Hine strolled through the Carpathian Mountains, he too encountered a thunderstorm. As the lightning flashed and the thunder rolled through the mountain range, his mind went to the Russian hymn that he had heard and that had become so dear to him. English verses began to form in his mind, verses that were suggested by portions of the Russian translation. Some time later a second verse was written as Hine roamed through the forests of Romania with some of the young people of that region. A third verse was written before returning to England.

In 1948, Stuart Hine and David Griffiths visited a camp in Sussex, England, where displaced Russians were being held. Only two in the whole camp knew Christ as Savior and would profess their belief. The testimony of one of them, and his anticipation of the second coming of Christ, inspired Hine to write the fourth stanza of his English version of the hymn.

In his book, *Not You, But God,* Hine presents two additional, optional verses that he copyrighted in 1953, as a translation of the Russian version. Dr. J. Edwin Orr introduced Hine's "How Great Thou Art" in the United States in 1954. Three years later, it began its orbit around the world by way of the Billy Graham New York Crusade and has since touched the lives of millions.

I have in my possession a prized copy of "How Great Thou Art" in the Russian language. All four of the men who helped bring us this song—Boberg, the Swede; Von Glehn, the German;

Prokhanoff, the Russian; and Hine, the Englishman—carefully preserved its awesome message.

In a letter from his daughter, Sonia Hine, dated March 16, 1989, which I personally held in my hands and read, was the somber news that Stuart Hine had died peacefully in his sleep two days before. He was ninety-two years of age. His memorial service was held at the Gospel Hall on Martello Road, Walton-on-Naze, Essex, England, on March 23, at two o'clock in the afternoon. Thus, in quiet dignity, ended the life on earth of a man whose long years had been dedicated to serving the Lord.

Reflection

When you hear the thunders roll, see a beautiful sunrise or an ocean view, or hear the singing of a bird, be reminded, as was Stuart Hine and Carl Boberg before him, of the greatness of the God we serve. Be thankful for all of His kindness to you and me.

46

Harpooned by His Own Crew

Amazing Grace

Ephesians 2:1–18

*For by grace are ye saved through faith; and that
not of yourselves: it is the gift of God: not of works,
lest any man should boast.*

On the high seas in the mid-1700s, an angry sailor threw a
whaling harpoon at his own captain who had fallen overboard.
What on earth would have provoked such anger and mutinous
behavior? The captain, John Newton, was a wicked, loathsome,
and cruel taskmaster with little regard for his crew or the human cargo chained in the hold of his slave ship. The harpoon
caught Newton in his hip and he was hauled back on board,
much like a large fish. He would limp for the rest of his life.

Newton, born in London, England, in 1725, had been going
to sea since age ten after only three years of formal schooling.
His first voyage was to the Mediterranean region with his father, captain of the ship. This seemed to be the only way the
older Newton knew how to care for his young son, whose mother
had died shortly before his seventh birthday.

Until his mother's death he had learned Scripture passages,
poems, and hymns at her knee. Most of her time, he later re-
vealed, was spent with his care and education. By his own testimony, at age four he could readily read "in any common book."

His early background and training were soon repressed as he associated with older, hardened sailors aboard his father's ship. The result was that he grew to be more wretched than almost anyone with whom he associated. His lifestyle led to rebellion, desertion, public floggings, abuse, destitution, and near drowning.

Once, while in the employ of a slave trader, he became ill and was left on the coast of Africa in the charge of a woman who locked him away and very nearly starved him to death. Only the kindness of the slaves in chains kept him alive as they shared with him morsels of their meager allotment of food.

Often, while enduring these horrid experiences, he thought back to his mother's instruction, striving to bring himself to a more religious state, but to no avail. He would read from the Bible, especially on Sundays. Each time, afterward, he would lapse into an even more wicked state, and would try to influence others to join him in his sinful disregard for things holy and decent. While in this condition Newton seemed to be totally unaware of God's marvelous grace in sparing his life time and again.

He was made the captain of his own ship at a very early age. And after a particularly harrowing experience during a violent storm at sea, when he despaired of life, Newton began to earnestly seek a right relationship with God. He had been reading *Imitation of Christ* by Thomas à Kempis. Apparently the book had a profound influence on his thinking.

Sometime later, while on a small island off the coast of North Africa, sick and alone, he experienced the amazing grace that he would later so eloquently write about.

The following is part of his written account: "Weak and delirious, I arose from my bed and crept to a secluded part of the island; there I found a renewed liberty to pray. I made no more resolves, but cast myself before the Lord to do with me as He should please. I was enabled to hope and believe in a crucified Savior. The burden was removed from my conscience." Newton, at that time and by God's grace, began a new life.

He married his sweetheart of many years and began to study

for the ministry, later becoming the pastor of a small church in Olney, England. While there he wrote many hymns and sacred songs. In 1779 he published a collection titled *The Olney Hymns,* one of which was "Amazing Grace." The captivating melody to which the lyrics are sung was written some fifty years later.

> Amazing grace, how sweet the sound,
> That saved a wretch like me!
> I once was lost, but now am found,
> Was blind, but now I see.
>
> Through many dangers, toils and snares,
> I have already come.
> 'Tis grace hath brought me safe thus far,
> And grace will lead me home.

Remember the harpooning incident? Well, Newton later said, "Each limp is a constant reminder of God's grace to this wretched sinner." He passed away at age 82. Following are the first few lines of his epitaph, written by his own hand and, according to his instructions, inscribed on a simple slab of marble and mounted near his burial place.

> John Newton, clerk, once an infidel and libertine,
> a servant of slaves in Africa,
> was by the rich mercy of our Lord and Savior, Jesus Christ
> preserved, restored, pardoned
> and appointed to preach the faith he had long
> labored to destroy.

Reflection

The miracle of amazing grace was experienced in a profound, dramatic fashion by the famous hymn writer himself. And you, too, can experience that grace!

47

He Wouldn't Do It for Money

What a Friend We Have in Jesus

Romans 15:1–7

We then that are strong ought to bear the infirmities of the weak, and not to please ourselves.

𝒯he town is Port Hope, Canada. A monument is being erected, not for the leading citizen who just died, but for a poor, unselfish, working man who gave most of his life and energy to help those who couldn't repay him.

Joseph Scriven was born in Dublin, Ireland, in 1819. He entered Trinity College in Dublin, but after a short time left and joined the army. His health was not good enough for him to be an active soldier, so his military career was cut short, and he reentered college and earned his degree.

In this youth, Ireland had the prospect of a great citizen with high ideals and great aspirations. He was engaged to a lovely lass who had promised to share his exalted dreams. On the eve of their wedding her body was pulled from a pond into which she had fallen and drowned. Young Scriven never overcame the shock. Although a college graduate and ready to embark on a brilliant career, he took to wandering to try to forget his sorrow. His travels took him to Port Hope, Canada, in 1844—at the age of twenty-five—where he spent the last forty-one of his sixty-six years. He became a very devout Christian.

His beliefs, as a member of the Plymouth Brethren church, led him to do servile labor for poor widows and sick people. He often served for no wages and was regarded by the people of the community as a kind man, but one who was an eccentric. Yet he fell in love again and planned to marry a wonderful, young Canadian woman. Again, tragedy came their way and she died after contracting pneumonia.

It was not known that Scriven had any poetic gifts until a short time before his death. A friend, who was sitting with him in an illness, discovered a poem that he had written to his mother in a time of sorrow, not intending that anyone else should see it. He had titled it "Pray Without Ceasing." The friend inquired who had written the poem, to which Scriven replied, "The Lord and I did it between us." He was not able, financially, to go to see his mother, but he thought the poem would, perhaps, bring some comfort to her in her time of need.

The friend who discovered Scriven's verses was responsible for having it published in a book of poems, *Hymns and Other Verses.*

> What a friend we have in Jesus,
> All our sins and griefs to bear!
> What a privilege to carry
> Everything to God in prayer!
> Oh, what peace we often forfeit,
> Oh, what needless pain we bear,
> All because we do not carry
> Everything to God in prayer.

The poem was later set to music by a talented musician of the day, Charles Converse, and titled "What a Friend We Have in Jesus." It is said to be one of the first song that many missionaries teach their converts. In the polls taken to determine the popularity of hymns and gospel songs, "What a Friend We Have in Jesus" always rates very high.

One morning in 1886, Scriven's body was pulled from Rice Lake in Ontario. It was not known exactly why he died in the water. Scriven will be long remembered as the man who helped others when they couldn't help themselves. From reading this and other narratives in this book, it can be concluded that the overriding philosophy in Christianity can be summed up in one word—others. We come back to it over and over again. Anything done for Christ must be done for others.

Reflection

Prayer, as presented in this song, is the most powerful force available to Christians everywhere. Any person who neglects the opportunity to commune with God and to draw on His resources will not show much growth in his or her faith. Reaffirm your commitment to pray more.

48

Nothing Short of Total Commitment

I Surrender All

Romans 12:1-15

*I beseech you therefore, brethren, by the mercies of
God, that ye present your bodies a living sacrifice,
holy, acceptable unto God, which is your
reasonable service.*

One of the most widely used songs in Christendom and its composer are the subjects of this story. It is probably one of the three most often used invitation songs in churches across the United States and many other countries. It ranks in popularity with "Just As I Am" and "Have Thine Own Way."

Of late, along with other "classic" gospel songs, it is being presented more and more to those with a love for Southern Gospel Music. At least one CD—made up solely of "classic hymns . . . quartet-style"—features Southern Gospel favorites such as Ernie Haase, and singers from such groups as the Nelons, Brian Free and Assurance, Gold City, Greater Vision, Old Time Gospel Hour Quartet, the Southern Brothers, LordSong, Cumberland Quartet, the Paynes, the Hoskins Family, and others.

Our songwriter, Dr. Judson W. Van DeVenter, was born in Monroe County in the state of Michigan on December 5, 1855. He was educated in the public schools of Dundee, Michigan, and at Hillsdale College, also in Michigan, graduating in 1875. He became a Christian at age seventeen and joined the Methodist Church. As he grew older he studied drawing and painting under a well-known German teacher. He said, "To help me financially, I taught school and, eventually, became supervisor of art in the public schools of Sharon, Pennsylvania."

Dr. Al Smith in his book, *Hymn Histories,* quotes Van DeVenter as saying, "It was during this period [teaching art in the public schools] that a revival was held in the First Methodist Church of which I was a member." Van DeVenter was a personal worker in the meetings and became extremely involved in the services.

Not long after that revival effort he was licensed as a lay preacher. The Lord blessed his efforts and he saw many souls born into the family of God. He felt a strong urge from the Lord to give up his teaching and enter the field of evangelism full-time, but he remained unyielding. His love of art was too strong—he wanted to be an outstanding artist. For five years this battle raged in his breast. Finally he came to the end of his will and surrendered, fully and completely, to the will of the Lord. He said, "It was then that a new day was ushered into my life. I became an evangelist and discovered that deep down in my soul was hidden a talent hitherto unknown to me. God had hidden a song in my heart and, touching a tender chord, He caused me to sing songs I had never sung before."

While in the home of George Sebring in East Palestine, Ohio, and while reflecting on his most important decision, he wrote his famous "I Surrender All."

> All to Jesus I surrender,
> All to Him I freely give;
> I will ever love and trust Him,
> In His presence daily live.

Chorus:
I surrender all, I surrender all,
All to Thee, my blessed Savior,
I surrender all.

All to Jesus, I surrender,
Humbly at His feet I bow,
Worldly pleasures all forsaken,
Take me, Jesus, take me now.

All to Jesus I surrender,
Make me Savior, wholly Thine;
May Thy Holy Spirit fill me,
May I know Thy pow'r divine.

Reflection

Nothing brings greater and more complete happiness into the heart of a Christian than the total surrender of one's self to the will of God.

49

Of Infinite Worth

His Eye Is on the Sparrow

Matthew 10:28-42

*Are not two sparrows sold for a farthing? and one
of them shall not fall on the ground without your
Father. . . . Fear ye not therefore, ye are of more
value than many sparrows.*

"God Will Take Care of You" was a wonderful lyric that came
from the pen of Mrs. Civilla D. Martin, a Canadian. That song,
however, was by no means her most famous. After her education in the schools of Nova Scotia she became a school teacher.
Before long she had met and married Dr. William Martin, an
evangelist and musician of sorts, and joined him in his itinerant work. Her poem, "God Will Take of You" was written for
her husband who set it to music. Although she had written
poetry for a number of years, it was the success of this song
that gave her some idea that God could use her poetic ability.

Early into the 1900s, Mrs. Martin heard of a dear friend who
had been overtaken with a severe state of depression. She became quite burdened for her friend and left their home, lo-
cated on the campus of a Bible school in Johnson City, New
York, and made her way by train to see the lady who lived in
Elmira, New York.

While there, Mrs. Martin told her friend of an incident that had happened a short time earlier when she experienced God's protecting hand during an illness. She hoped that the story would be an encouragement to the depressed soul.

After hearing the story her friend said, "You know, I shouldn't worry, should I? We are promised in the Bible that God watches over the little sparrows." Mrs. Martin agreed, "He surely does." They then had a little time of rejoicing over God's wonderful watchful care and protection.

The journey back home was made shorter for Mrs. Martin by the satisfying realization that she had helped her friend. When she arrived home, she sat down and penned the words to one of the most beautiful and famous of all the gospel songs, "His Eye Is on the Sparrow." Her husband tried his hand at writing a musical setting, but they were not at all satisfied with it and sent the poem to Charles H. Gabriel, a famous songwriter, and asked him to write some fitting music for it. He did so, and his melody has been the vehicle that carried Mrs. Martin's poem around the world. It was first sung by Charles M. Alexander during the Torrey-Alexander revival in Royal Albert Hall in England in 1905.

"His Eye Is on the Sparrow" became a signature song for Ethel Waters, who sang it on a number of occasions in the Billy Graham Crusades and on several national television programs.

The magnificent and encouraging lyrics of this song are presented here in their entirety:

> Why should I feel discouraged,
> Why should the shadows come,
> Why should my heart be lonely,
> And long for heaven and home?
> When Jesus is my portion,
> My constant Friend is He,
> His eye is on the sparrow,
> And I know He watches me.

Chorus:

I sing because I'm happy,
I sing because I'm free,
For His eye is on the sparrow,
And I know He watches me.

"Let not your heart be troubled,"
His tender Word I hear.
And resting on His goodness,
I lose my doubts and fears;
Tho' by the path He leadeth,
But one step I may see.
His eye is on the sparrow,
And I know He watches me.

Whenever I am tempted,
Whenever clouds arise,
When songs give place to sighing,
When hope within me dies,
I draw the closer to Him,
From care He sets me free,
His eye is on the sparrow,
And I know He watches me.

Reflection

None of us would ever worry over a single problem if we possessed a deep-seated assurance that our heavenly Father cares more for us than for all of His other earthly creatures. He cares more for me than I am able to care for myself.

50

What Does This Tune Say?

Blessed Assurance

1 John 5:1–13

*These things have I written unto you that believe
on the name of the Son of God; that ye may know
that ye have eternal life, and that ye may believe on
the name of the Son of God.*

*F*anny Crosby is one of the most notable names in hymnology. She penned more than eight thousand songs in her lifetime, which spanned nearly a century—she died in her ninety-fifth year—and most of it was spent in blindness. Not even the loss of her eyesight could render defeat to this courageous soul.

She was born Frances Jane Crosby in Putnam County, New York, on March 24, 1820. A doctor, lacking proper medical knowledge, applied a mustard plaster poultice to her eyes when she was only six weeks old, robbing her of her sight. Yet she grew to be a cheerful, happy soul with a marvelous attitude. She accepted her handicap with an unusual amount of courage.

She often said, "I have a jewel—content." When she was only eight years of age she wrote,

> O what a happy soul am I,
> Although I cannot see,

> I am resolved that in this world
> Contented I will be.
> How many blessings I enjoy
> That other people don't.
> To weep and sigh because I'm blind,
> I cannot and I won't.

At age fifteen she wrote,

> His purposes will ripen fast,
> Unfolding every hour.
> The bud may have a bitter taste,
> But sweet will be the flower.

During her fifteenth year she entered the New York Institute for the Blind, where she made such an impressive record that after graduation she was asked to teach at the Institute. She did so for eleven years. She told S. Trevena Jackson her little "love story," which he recorded in *Fanny Crosby's Story of Ninety-four Years,* published by Fleming H. Revell in 1915:

> Some people seem to forget that blind girls have just as great a faculty for loving, and do love just as much and just as truly as those who have their sight. When I was about twenty a gifted young man by the name of Alexander Van Alstyne came to our Institute. He was also blind and very fond of classic literature and theological lore, but made music a specialty. After hearing several of my poems he became deeply interested in my work; and I after listening to his sweet strains of music became interested in him. Thus we soon became very much concerned for each other. . . . I placed my right hand on his left and called him "Van." Then it was that two happy lovers sat in silence while the sunbeams danced around their heads, and the golden curtains of

day drew in their light. Van took up the harp of love, and drawing his fingers over the golden chords, sang to me the song of a true lover's heart. From that hour two lives looked on a new universe, for love met love, and all the world was changed.

We were no longer blind, for the light of love showed us where the lilies bloomed, and where the crystal waters find the moss-mantled spring. On March the fifth in the year 1858 we were united in marriage.

Now I am going to tell you something that only my closest friends know. I became a mother and knew a mother's love. God gave us a tender baby, but the angels came down and took our infant up to God and His throne. Van went home to his Father's house in the year 1902.

She wrote using her own name as well as many pseudonyms. It is estimated that in her lifetime she wrote more than eight thousand songs, and the story behind one of those songs is the subject at hand.

One day in 1873, Aunt Fanny, as she was affectionately called, was visiting with a friend, Mrs. Joseph Knapp, a musician of sorts and wife of the founder of Metropolitan Life Insurance Company. During their visit, Mrs. Knapp played a tune she had recently written, and then asked Fanny, "What does this tune say?" Fanny knelt in prayer, and as she prayed, the tune was played again. Suddenly she rose from her prayer and said, "It says, 'Blessed Assurance, Jesus is mine, Oh what a foretaste of glory divine!'" Fanny dictated verses to Mrs. Knapp who wrote them down, fitting them to the melody just as we hear it sung today.

> Blessed assurance, Jesus is mine!
> O what a foretaste of glory divine!
> Heir of salvation, purchase of God.
> Born of His Spirit, washed in His blood.

Chorus:

This is my story, this is my song,
Praising my Savior, all the day long,
This is my story, this is my song,
Praising my Savior, all the day long.

Other songs written by Fanny Crosby include, "Praise Him! Praise Him!" "Draw Me Nearer," "To God Be the Glory," and "Rescue the Perishing." She went to be with the Lord only a few short weeks before her ninety-fifth birthday. On her tombstone in Bridgeport, Connecticut, are these words from Jesus' remarks concerning the woman in Bethany: "She hath done what she could."

Reflection

No song is more meaningful than one that declares our relationship to the heavenly Father, and at the same time is a song of praise to Him.

Song Index

Author/Composer Index